Recollections Of Fenians And Fenianism

JAMES STEPHENS.

Frontispiece to Vol. II.

RECOLLECTIONS

OF

FENIANS AND FENIANISM

BY

JOHN O'LEARY

IN TWO VOLUMES

VOL. II.

WITH PORTRAITS

LONDON
DOWNEY & CO., LIMITED
12 YORK STREET, COVENT GARDEN
1896

CONTENTS.

RECOLLECTIONS

OF

Fenians and Fenianism.

CHAPTER I.

FINANCIAL TROUBLES—OUR CORRESPONDENT.

During these early weeks of the *Irish People* our difficulties were chiefly internal and financial, for as yet we had dealt little, if at all, with the current politics of the day, and so necessarily avoided controversy. But, if we had not trouble one way, we had it in a very acute form in another. Stephens had started the paper with some incredibly small sum of money in hand, and so, after a very few numbers had appeared, our funds fell short, and we had a weekly struggle to bring out each number, *en attendant* the coming in of money from subscriptions, advertisements, and the like, or the arrival of any funds from America. The burden of this trouble fell materially and morally mostly on Rossa and myself. Rossa, in that he was the manager, had naturally most to do, at least at this early stage of our existence, with the question of supplies, and, in point of fact, if I remember aright, he had to pay out of his own pocket for some weeks the current expenses of the paper, whereas I, having some permanent, as Rossa had some temporary, resources, was obliged to do without such scanty salary as had been assigned me, for the time being, and, indeed, I may be roughly said to have done without it till the end. But there is no need to go into any further details. We struggled on, and, though we had difficulties of a money kind all along, still the great trouble was at the beginning. Of course, if there was no money for the paper, there was none for the organization, and that, too, was necessarily starved during this period, which, however, was but a short time, for after a little the paper itself served as a sort of recruiting agency for the organization; was a natural channel of communication between its members, and kindled enthusiasm inside and outside the Fenian body. That was the gain. There was of course a loss. To the whole reading public it was soon inferentially evident enough that a secret body was spread over the country, having for its object the overthrow of English rule in Ireland. I do not know, however, that the loss was so great as it looks. Of course the Government was at all times aware of the existence of the conspiracy, and, I suppose, roughly, could feel its strength. But the question was not what the Government guessed or felt, but what it actually knew, and, as far as I can at all make out down to the present day, that was exceedingly little up to the loss of the so-called "documents" by Mr. Meehan, of the *Irish-American*, in 1865. But I am anticipating, and must return to the *Irish People*. There was one thing which after a time came to form a very important element in the paper, and that was its correspondence. In the beginning, and before the paper was started, there appears to have prevailed a notion among some clever and more or less literary young men, but notably young men in and about Skibbereen, that they were going to have a big inning in the new paper, as leading-article writers and the like. But after a time both they and we found that that theory would not work. We got no leading articles, but from the beginning we got some good letters, and as the paper went on, the letters grew greatly in numbers and importance, not in literary importance, for as literary performances they were most imperfect all along, but as truthful and fairly intelligent purveyors of news from their respective localities they were important all along and interesting very often. Not that several of these letters were not well written also, but that the value of them did not come from their form, but from their substance—from the facts they contained and the information they supplied of the sayings and doings of men all over the country. There were some half-dozen or more of these correspondents who wrote very well indeed and whose communications might often have taken the form of essays, leading articles, and the like, had they and we so chosen. The best of these, as a writer, I think, was a Kingstown schoolmaster, Hugh Byrne, who used to sign himself

"Hugo del Monte." Moynihan, one of the Skibbereen Phœnix men of whom I have spoken before, was also a very good writer in his way, having always a fair basis of thought beneath any literary structure he sought to erect. Harvey Birch, a Tipperary national teacher, of the name of Brohan, had a light and effective touch, and always something to say, as so also always had "De l'Abbaye," though with him there was mostly more in the matter than in the manner. But I cannot go on noticing, however cursorily, all our correspondents. They had their day and passed away, and, I fear, 'tis but few of them that I can bring into such small temporary notice as this book might give them. Some others I shall have to speak of as I go on, and as quarrels and controversies in which they have taken part arise. Many priests we had, after a time, among our correspondents, and they were mostly, though not always, among the most violent in tone, and very often the rashest in statement. But up to the period with which I am dealing just now we were not polemical, and priests, either as friends or enemies, had little to say to us.

CHAPTER II.

THE ROTUNDA AFFAIR—THE SULLIVANS.

THE era of combat may be said to have commenced for us with our thirteenth number, February 20th, 1864,* and I can perhaps do no better, in commencing some account of the first and worst of our quarrels, than quote the greater part of a short article in the paper of that date, entitled "The Albert Dodge." "We observed in *The Morning News* (a paper edited by Mr. A. M. Sullivan) of Thursday a sensational advertisement, headed in large capitals, and with notes of admiration—THE VOTE OF COLLEGE GREEN! GRATTAN EXPELLED FOR EVER! PRINCE ALBERT IN HIS STEAD!! PUBLIC MEETING IN THE ROTUNDA![1] and announcing that, on Monday evening next, The O'Donoghue and several other distinguished Irishmen would attend a meeting to reconsider the 'Recent Vote' of the Corporation, etc. Now, if the individuals, who are engaged in getting up this meeting, intend to confine themselves simply to the statue affair, we have nothing to say about the matter. They can use their pleasure, and have their meeting. But, if they

[1] The pretext for this meeting was the intention—real or supposed—of certain people to use the site of the Grattan statue for one to Prince Albert.

mean to take advantage of this sensation clap-trap, and surreptitiously foist a new parliamentary humbug upon us, we think the people should not stand a dodge of so brassy a complexion. We shall only add that all *earnest* nationalists, all practical workers, should meet on Monday evening next, and observe with vigilant eye the proceedings. They can then act according to circumstances."

The practical workers did meet on Monday, and did "act according to circumstances," though whether these circumstances quite justified their action is another matter. I thought not at the time, and rather incline to think not still, but that was by no means the opinion of Luby and most of the others amongst my co-religionists, as I shall have to show in speaking of a well-known article of Luby's, written for the next number of the paper. In the meantime, I may as well tell what the practical workers did on that Monday night.

They simply stormed the platform and swept all who were on it off it, and this without waiting for anything further than the taking of the chair by The O'Donoghue, and the endorsement by that gentleman, in the opening sentences of his speech, of "his esteemed friend and co-patriot, Mr. A. M. Sullivan." The meeting clearly would have nothing to do with Mr. Sullivan, and I still think they were right in their want of faith in that gentleman; but they might have taken some milder way of manifesting it.

But this was not Luby's opinion, nor that of the general body of the Fenians, and, consequently, in the next issue of the paper, Luby struck a note of triumph far too highly pitched to my taste, but still I let the thing pass, abdicating my editorship for the time being; for this matter was no way vital to me, and I could not give up my functions altogether merely because I thought the party were making something of a mountain out of a mole-hill. Here is the opening paragraph of the article. "On Monday night (February 22nd, 1864), in the Rotunda, the people of Dublin gained a glorious moral triumph. They consummated a noble act of public justice. They made manifest to the world that there is one thing above all which Irishmen will never tolerate, and that is, a felon-setter, acting the part of a patriot.[1] No shallow notions of false tolerance will ever prevail upon them to be guilty of base time-serving like this." There was certainly a great physical triumph, and that was something for the party of physical force; and there was a something moral certainly, if scarcely to be dignified with the name of triumph, in the *sæva indignatio* shown against felon-setters.

But to go on with the story of the Rotunda meetings and some of their more immediate consequences. I have not gone into the reasons assigned by Luby for the action of the Fenians and their sympathizers at the Rotunda, for I have had to treat the matter of felon-setting elsewhere,

[1] As I have said before, times have changed sadly since Luby wrote, and they are changing again as I write, and may have changed again before I have done with my reminiscences. I am not giving my recollections of these later times, and only allude to them in so far as they have any bearing upon that past with which I have directly to do.

and am dealing with it now mainly in connection with the polemics of the paper. Sometime in the week succeeding the first Rotunda meeting, a conference was arranged, by whom I know not now, between Kickham and myself on the one side and John Dillon and The O'Donoghue on the other, to see if we could not come to some terms as to the conditions on which the next meeting might be held, without any interruption on our part. We met on the Sunday, but came to no agreement. I mention this conference chiefly that I may say a word or two about The O'Donoghue, the "Young Chieftain," the "Chieftain of the Glens," the "Young Liberator," or whatever else he used to be called in the newspaper language of the day. This person was then a sort of idol, at least with the non-Fenian portion of the national party, though why it would be hard to make out, save that he was the nephew of O'Connell, and a man of good birth and some property, which he had by that time, however, nearly entirely frittered away. I do not know whether I ever saw that young gentleman before or after that particular Sunday; but what I then saw of him gave me the idea of a very poor creature indeed. As I had known John Dillon before, and as I knew that he was the person on his side with whom the decision rested, I naturally fell into talk with him, leaving Kickham to take care of the young Chieftain. And, if the matter were left to the last two, it would be easy indeed, for it was soon evident that Kickham could get the hero of the glens to agree to anything, at least for the time being, but his assent or agreement, or what seemed to be such, counted for very little, for it was immediately nullified by the merest dissenting word or gesture on the part of Dillon. I soon saw, on the contrary, that Dillon would come to no agreement, and so I went on talking with him after a time on other things, and scarcely exchanged a word, after our introduction, with the Chieftain.[1]

The second Rotunda meeting was held, then, a week after the first, but it was only by a *façon de parler* that it could be called a public one. People were admitted only by ticket, and after very careful scrutiny of the ticket too, and, while the meeting was a picked and selected body of some hundreds, all the approaches to the meeting were lined by thousands of highly hostile spectators, held in check by a large force of police, so that, as I said at the time, "The O'Donoghue and his esteemed friend, Mr. Sullivan, fought their way to fame, through files of policemen, on last Monday."[2]

[1] The O'Donoghue, when he had ceased to be a nationalist altogether and became some sort of nondescript West-Briton, showed very much more ability than he had previously done, but that ability seems to have lain nearly altogether in the talking line, and, in any case, he neither then nor at any time seems to have shown any character at all, either in the English or the French acceptation of the word. But, though he was a prominent figure in Irish politics for a good while, he is scarcely worth the slight amount of attention I have given him here.

[2] All the facts about this second Rotunda meeting are to be found in the *Freeman's Journal, Irish Times, Saunders' Newsletter*, and other papers of the day. The *Freeman* says that "so jealous were the promoters of the meeting of the privilege of *entrée* that the doors leading to the Round Room were but rarely more than half open, and even then they were guarded jealously and efficiently by a posse of ticket-takers." It also tells us that "large bodies of police were stationed at different points of the immediate neighbourhood of the Rotunda, while some of them co-operated with the ticket-takers." But it is needless to enter into any details of

But enough about these Rotunda meetings. They made a great noise at the time, and much angry controversy arose out of them. But all that concerns us but little just now. Their main significance lay in the fact that they showed the strength of the Fenian element in Dublin. Not that I at all know that the thousands who thronged the streets on the day of the second meeting were Fenians, but largely Fenian they must have been, and in entire sympathy with Fenian objects, in so far as they understood them, they clearly showed themselves to be. Indeed from this time forward the weight of opinion in favour of Fenianism seemed to be constantly growing, or rather it was perhaps that Fenianism was getting better known, for it is the experience of what is now a pretty long life with me that the Fenian spirit is ever present in Ireland, and needs at any time but a little organization to make it burst into renewed activity. We hear constantly of the diminution of disaffection in Ireland, and even of late we have been hearing of the growth of affection, but all that is very idle talk. Disaffected we have been, disaffected we are, and disaffected we shall remain, till the English let go their grip of us.[1] Anyway, at the time

this meeting, which, whatever it was, or whatever significance it might have, was certainly in no sense public, but, on the contrary, took effective means to show that the public was opposed to it and its supposed objects.

[1] Not merely loosen their hold on us. I am writing what I take to be historical, and what is certainly autobiographical, and do not care to be more prospectively political than I can help. I cannot, therefore, here or now change from figures of speech to facts of Government, but there is not the slightest use in concealing from any class of Englishmen that, until they have brought

of which I speak, disaffection was deepening day by day, hopes were growing high, and everything so far had gone well, save that still, as all along up to this, the progress of the organization was much impeded by the absence of the proverbial sinews of war. Happily, however, about the time to which I have now come, or shortly after, things began to improve financially also, and, as I have mentioned at an earlier stage of my narrative, it was during the existence of the *Irish People* that by far the largest part—never however large—of the American fund flowed in upon the Fenian exchequer.

themselves to see that the less they have to do with us the better it will be for them and us, they have practically learned little or nothing about us.

CHAPTER III.

KICKHAM—THE BISHOP OF CHICAGO.

BUT to go back to the *Irish People*. In speaking of the paper last, I dwelt somewhat upon a series of articles by Kickham, giving a sort of bird's-eye view of the national, or so-called national, politics for the dozen years or so that had just elapsed. Now, he took to dealing more directly with the politics of the day, and especially in their politico-ecclesiastical aspects, for, as I said before, we left this side of things mostly to Kickham, who, while invariably, I think, *suaviter in modo*, was certainly always *fortiter in re*. In the seventeenth number of the paper (March 19th, 1864) appeared, I think, the first of these articles, headed "The Chicago Fair Denunciation." [1] This had reference to a long letter from John O'Mahony, which had appeared in our previous number, dealing with the anti-Fenian denunciations of Dr. Duggan, the Bishop of Chicago. "We notice that Bishop Duggan," says Kickham, "by way of proving

[1] This fair, which was rather what we call a bazaar, had been making a great stir in our columns for months. Its avowed object was to collect money for revolutionary objects, and this it was aided in doing by all sorts of contributions from Ireland, mostly of trifling money value, but always having some sort of interest, chiefly of the pathetic kind, for the poor exiles of Erin.

that he was right in denouncing the Fenians, told his flock that the Society had been denounced by Dr. Cullen; while Dr. Cullen, by way of strengthening his case against the devoted Fenians, told his flock that they were denounced by Bishop Duggan." The article goes on to say that people are getting more than a little tired. "It is indeed hard for Christian men and women, assembled for the worship of their Maker, to be obliged to listen, week after week, to denunciations of their neighbours, whose lives, they know, would bear comparison with those of any other portion of the community." Kickham goes on to argue, as O'Mahony had done, that the attitude of the priests towards the Irish trouble was quite different from that which they took up in the case of Poland. "And the Irishman is banned by the same voice which calls down a blessing on the Pole. Our people are melting away. Our homesteads are levelled to the ground. Hunger and despair sit by the poor man's hearth. He looks into the pale faces of his children, and, thinking of the workhouse—the hot-bed of crime—wishes that they had never been born. There is but one hope to cheer him—the hope that the tyranny that made him what he is, and doomed him to a pauper's grave, will be struck down. What must be the feelings of this man's heart when he thinks that the dignitaries of his church, who know not want and nakedness themselves, are the allies of his tyrant? And while those who would prepare to grapple with the despoiler, and save a suffering people from destruction, are vilified and denounced—the base recreant, the placebeggar, the political mountebank, the ermined perjurer,[1] the very exterminator—all these are courted and smiled upon and blessed."

Here Kickham strikes a true note, and strikes it firmly. There may, perhaps, be a little rhetorical exaggeration in the manner of expression, but that does not seriously detract from the substantial truth of what is said. The priests, in all later movements, might be said, roughly speaking, to have been on the side that was neither the honest nor the national one. They were almost universally for O'Connell,[2] with his accompanying Dillon Browns, Somerses, Reynoldses and the like, as against the Young Irelanders, they were largely with Keogh and Sadlier against Lucas and Duffy, and now they were taking a side again, and one which I think the universal national feeling of the country would now hold to have been the wrong one.

It might have been fairly open to them to have opposed the Young Irelanders and Fenians on the grounds of expediency, but they always went much farther than that, seldom failing to attribute the worst motives to their adversaries, and making charges

[1] The reader of the present day may need to be told that the allusion in the text is to the then notorious and always infamous Judge Keogh, the whole latter part of the passage, indeed, contrasting the way the priests treat certainly roguish agitators with their conduct towards only possibly foolish rebels.

[2] They had an excuse in this case which was totally absent in the others. O'Connell had certainly served Catholicity and striven to serve nationality, and the priests might have been excused for sticking to him *per Fas aut nefas*. But they need not have taken to his hideous tail and stuck to it long after the head was gone.

against their private and public lives which history has in no way substantiated.

Henceforward, until the Government swept down upon us and put an end, for the time being, to us and our politics, we waged a steady war against what came to be called "Priests in Politics."[1] We never, of course, in the least denied the absolute right of a priest, any more than of a lawyer, or a doctor, to hold any political opinion he liked, but we did wholly refuse to consider that a political opinion gained any weight or force from being held by a priest. On the contrary, we held that priests were likely to be worse politicians than other men, for many reasons, but especially in that they had less knowledge of the world, coming out of Maynooth and elsewhere, to take often at once an active part in the political life of the country, without any political training whatever. In all our polemics with the priests we had the aid of priests, but still such help as we got from them, though useful in its way, scarcely affects the general question, the exceptions here as elsewhere only serving to prove the rule. In our nineteenth number there was a long letter signed "A Country Priest," and in our twentieth there is another long one signed "An Irish Priest," and addressed to the Irish-Americans.

[1] A reason we never put forward in the old times, I think, against "Priests in Politics" was their ignorance, though, of course, it has often been alleged against them by their Protestant Conservative adversaries. I, however, personally think that priests are, as a rule, on a lower level of culture than lawyers, doctors, and others of the so-called educated classes.

In the same number of the paper Kickham takes up the cudgels a second time against the Bishop of Chicago, who had been entertaining a deputation of Fenians with his views upon various matters, telling them, among other things, "that it was a violation of the laws of the Catholic Church to entertain the idea of freeing Ireland by force of arms." I take this on the authority of Kickham, who is naturally rather astonished as to where or how the Bishop found that doctrine, and goes on to say by way of comment what puts rather shortly one of our contentions. "They (the priests) appear to make no distinction between purely spiritual and mere temporal matters. What they disapprove of as men they think they have a right to anathematize as the successors of the Apostles. Sincere and enlightened Catholics justly apprehend great danger to religion from this jumbling together of religion and politics. The Irish priest assumes an authority over his flock which the clergy of other Catholic countries never dream of assuming." Kickham goes on to give reasons why it was natural this state of things should have existed in the past, but thinks it out of place in the then present; still it has projected itself into the actual present, and is, I fear, destined to survive many futures still in the womb of time.

how true 1887

CHAPTER IV.

NOCTIS HIBERNICÆ—REUNIONS OF THE STAFF.

I HAVE told how the daily routine of office work brought me into more or less constant communication with Luby, Kickham and Mulcahy, but now I have to speak of another, an easier, and a more intimate intercourse, which, if not constant, was constantly recurring. It was the habit of the literary staff[1] of the paper to meet at my lodgings on the nights (Fridays) we went to press. Kickham was always present, Luby and Mulcahy mostly,

[1] The chief of these of whom I have a very vivid recollection was Dr. Sigerson, for the intercourse between us, which began then, has gone on intermittingly ever since, being constant of late years, and is pretty sure to last till one or other of us shall go to join the majority. I need scarcely say that Sigerson was not a Fenian, and knew little more about our plans or designs than could be gathered from Irish and American papers. A Nationalist he, of course, was then as now, as he often showed in our columns, but still oftener in those of the *Irishman*, in vigorous and numerous prose and verse. Sigerson, like nearly all the Irishmen I know, has most likely committed more or less misprision of treason during the course of his life, but treason or treason-felony most certainly never, though to what height of sedition his famous "Holocaust" may have reached, or whether it may have bordered on the higher offence, not being a lawyer, I do not pretend to tell. Enough that at this time that friendship of his for Kickham and myself commenced which went on till the death of the one and is likely to last for the life of the other.

and Stephens but occasionally. Others there were also. My sisters were often in town, and when with me, of course, formed part of the gathering, and a younger brother, a medical student who was staying with me during the greater part of the time, was necessarily with us often too. Outsiders there were, too, but of course still more irregularly and erratically.

At these convivial meetings we talked of everything and nothing, literature, politics, gossip and, of course, much "shop." The paper and all that concerned it being ever present to the minds of all of us. It is not easy for me to recall these *noctes cœnæque* at this distance of time, having little of that marvellous gift of memory possessed by my friend Luby. I might indeed draw upon Luby's rich stores of recollection here as elsewhere, but there must be some limit to the measure of my obligations to him, and hereafter, as before, I shall only make use of him where my knowledge fails, which can only be in slight matters for the future, and not where my memory is not full.

But alas! many things I remember but too well. "Sorrow's crown of sorrow is remembering happier things." There are no doubt "Pleasures of Memory" for all of us as well as the late Mr. Rogers, but they must be faint when not largely mingled with the "Pleasures of Hope." And where can hope come in here for me? I cannot call the dead to life. All of whom I spoke above are not dead, but the nearest and dearest are, and there are for me, humanly speaking, no possibilities of any future, which can in the least make up for, or make me in the least forgetful of, that past. Even with the living it is mostly altogether a matter of the past. Oceans divide me from Luby and Mulcahy, and communication, either personal or by letter, is rare, though mostly (always when it is personal) pleasant when it comes.

Luby I have spoken of oftener than anybody else in the course of my story. He, I am happy to say, is not only living but very much alive indeed, triumphant over the past—his and my past, active (mentally at least) in the present, and bating no jot of heart or hope for the future. He is[1] now "the old man eloquent" and, I think, in most ways more remarkable than in the olden days which I am trying to recall. But certainly wonderful enough he was then too. A perfect hurricane of life (on the surface at least and to the superficial eye), for ever hurling forth a tornado of speech. Anyway, in those days as in these he was the pleasantest of companions, peppery indeed as well as spicy at times, though never for long, and ever with a full and flowing tide of conversation, which, though often vehement and obstreperous, and occasionally violent and aggressive, was never in the least tinged with any hue of malignity. Vain he was then as now, but with that vanity which has no touch of envy in it, and so nearly always amuses and seldom or ever irritates. Anyway, a pleasanter or more

[1] Luby has now reached the limit of age assigned to man by the Psalmist, but I think, as I certainly hope, he has many years before him. I do not particularly love the land he lives in, as indeed neither does he, and my hopes are but faint of seeing him in the land we both love, but there or here I hope to see him and his at least once more before I die.

resourceful companion than Luby was in those olden days it is impossible to conceive. He had words at will, as Carlyle is said to have said of certain Young Irelanders, but, unlike most voluble men, he had always plenty of thought behind the words.[1]

But to pass away, for the time at least, from the merely social or convivial to the serious and political side of Luby. It was chiefly through him that I kept in touch with the movement during the greater part of this time. He saw somewhat more of Stephens than I did, for officially I had little or nothing to do with him during the greater part of the time, and socially I was feeling less inclined to cultivate him, and Luby was necessarily obliged to be somewhat more in communication with him, while all along he was in nearly as direct, intimate, and extensive communication with the chief men of the organization as Stephens himself. Through him then I heard and knew of everything, and from him I could of course always rely upon getting at the truth and the facts of the case, so far as they were known, but as to the interpretation to be put on these facts, the hopes or fears to be gathered from them, there my confidence was very much less, for my temperament was very different. I mention these things about Luby and myself in connection with those social gatherings, for it was at them chiefly, I think, that we talked over matters, as Luby

[1] Luby among his other gifts has a very great turn for speculation, and a very competent knowledge of metaphysical writers, having a special cult for his great countryman Berkeley. I have thought it necessary to say so much because Luby's writings, so far as known to me, show little, if any, of this side of his mind.

often remained on with me, after the others had left, very far into the small hours of the morning. Of course I saw him often at the office too, but there I was mostly busy with the affairs of the paper; anyway, much I saw of him somewhere at all times. As I have also said before, we nearly always thought and felt much in the same way about Irish men and things, though rather more similarly about the latter than the former, and always with the difference that, while Luby was nearly always hopeful, I was always very much the reverse. It would then be more correct to say that, speculatively, we thought and felt alike, but sometimes, as in the case of the Rotunda meetings, we differed very considerably in the practical way of looking at things.

But I am getting away from these reunions of mine, if not in person, in a sense in spirit, for generally we were not only more literary than political in our topics, but mostly too, if I remember aright, we were, even when political, rather more retrospective than present or prospective in our talk. Naturally we spoke much of the Young Irelanders, as we felt that of course we were in a measure the outcome of them and their movement, though with us and our movement they would (naturally enough perhaps) have nothing to do. I do not think now that we took sufficiently[1] charitable views of the

[1] Kickham and I thought all along a little differently on this matter from Luby, and of course altogether differently from Stephens. Stephens never had a good word for the Young Irelanders after his first visit to America, and Luby was very much irritated, if not embittered, by the action of some of them in the M'Manus funeral business. We, on the contrary, had not

motives or conduct of these gentlemen, though of the goodness of the motives of two of them, Mr. Smith O'Brien and Mr. John Martin, I had never any doubt, however little I thought their conduct at the time consistent with their own past.[1] If we were the fools they seemed to take us to be then, what had they been but a very few years before? It was open to them to confess the errors of their past, but that they did not do, or to allege some changes in the times unfavourable to an insurrectionary policy, and this they did, but I think with altogether inconclusive results. It was said that the population of Ireland had decreased, but that did not make such a great difference; neither did the increased population of England, nor the improvement in weapons of war, though for something all these certainly counted. *Per contra,* we did not mean to rush into a fight suddenly and without arms in our hands. We had

been thrown into personal antagonism with them, and for that as for other reasons did not share in the personal animosities of Stephens or Luby.

[1] Of others of the Young Irelanders then, as now, I thought differently. In Darcy McGee's speech, in Wexford, I think, I saw nothing then and I see nothing now but blatant blackguardism or corrupt villainy. Of Mr. John Dillon, who was perhaps intellectually the most eminent Young Irelander then in Ireland, I thought then, as now, that he had simply either lost faith in Nationality altogether, or, like his more prominent but less distinguished son, had always been more Agrarian than National. I have been told, by a friend and a distinguished Irishman, that I have been very unjust to McGee, and it is of course possible that I have, but I cannot see it. I fully recognize the great intellectual merits of the man, and his very considerable literary services—which, however, have been very much over-estimated by Ferguson and others—to his country, but I cannot see anything in him, politically or morally, that was not low, and even base.

large possible resources, unknown to the men of '48, in the shape of men and money in America, and the absolute certainty, long before the end came, that the Irish soldiers in the English army could be reckoned upon, not for England, but for Ireland.

But, if we must necessarily have talked much politics, directly or indirectly, on these occasions, we, as I have said, talked still more of literature and other things. Especially did Kickham talk, and provoke talk, about books and their writers; not that he knew a great deal about either, but he certainly felt intensely about both. And the one thing he could always throw into his talk, as he has spread it broadcast over his books, was feeling, and it is needless to tell any of his readers, who must be numerous amongst mine, how profoundly Irish that feeling was. Many other intellectual and moral gifts he had too, though this matter of feeling may be said to form the "note" of his character. Humour he had in abundance, and imagination too, for without a fair share of this last he could neither be the poet, which he certainly was, nor the novelist, which he is much better known to be. But what was not known then, and what to the general public is not well known yet, was that he had very considerable reasoning powers, and one of the soundest judgments I have found among such public men as I have known. The strength of this judgment, as the strength of his will, became, however, far clearer to me in times long after those of which I am writing now, for I fear that in the olden times, while I liked him much and felt his literary gift to be a very real one, I did not value him on the whole at all as highly as he deserved, feeling most likely some of the reading man's contempt for the comparatively unread man, and not realizing fully, though perhaps dimly suspecting, how very much he surpassed myself, and indeed I think all other men I have ever known, in that most vital knowledge—the knowledge of his own countrymen.

But why go on with this analysis of Kickham and his character? I have, I fear, said either too little or to much; too little to let the reader know all I think or feel about the dead patriot, and too much when I come to think that my main business is not with Kickham, but with that much less interesting personage, myself, or with the first only in relation to the second. But still nothing is more natural than that his name should be often in my mouth, for it is almost always coupled with mine in the minds of the Irish people, whenever that people wake up to the consciousness that Kickham once lived, and taught, and wrought, and that I, happily or unhappily, am still in this world, though perhaps scarcely of it.[1]

Neither need I dwell any longer on these *noctes Hibernicæ* of ours. They were pleasant while they lasted, but like most pleasant things they did not last long. It gives me now little but pain to try to recall them to memory, and I fear that the picture I have been able to set before the reader is at best but faintly

[1] As I said before, the people here seem to have nearly altogether forgotten Luby, but I feel confident they will know much about him long after he and I and others have gone to our graves.

outlined and somewhat blurred. "The gentle poet of Slievnamon" has long since gone from among us, and alas! so too has she[1] who sung of him, and now, as I write, another and a younger,[2] one of the brightest and best of God's creatures, and one very dear to Kickham, my sister, and myself in these later years, has been taken to "where the wicked cease from troubling and the weary are at rest." Luby, Mulcahy, myself, and some few others of that old set still survive, but I of late seem to myself as if I were living in a graveyard.[3]

I hasten back then to another past which I feel is not altogether dead, and cannot die while there is still life in the old land. You may forget it for a time, and even come to condemn it, or at least pretend to do so, in blatant balderdash about union of hearts and the like; but all that passes away, and you are for ever brought back to that past, and the other pasts out of which it arose.

[1] My sister. [2] Rose Kavanagh.

[3] When I came back to Ireland, after some twenty years' absence, I was soon made to feel in many ways as if I belonged to another age and another time. By certain youthful admirers of mine, I found I was sometimes grandly spoken of as "the veteran patriot" and familiarly known as "the old man," and yet I was then (towards the close of '84) little over fifty-four years old.

CHAPTER V.

SPREAD OF THE ORGANIZATION IN THE WEST AND THE NORTH.

THE organization at the end of '63 and the beginning of '64 had already reached considerable proportions, but through all this last year it went on gathering strength and force in all directions. During the earlier years of its existence it was to a large extent confined to certain parts of Leinster and Munster, places most easily reached by Dublin or Cork agents, and most easily governed from these two centres. This limitation of our activity, in the earlier times and indeed for a good while, was, as I have said, altogether owing to our lack of funds. Moving about, even in the humblest way and with the most careful measuring of means, still always involves the expenditure of money, more or less as the case may be, and, as I have shown, in the earlier years there was little or no money at all; in fact, not more than was sufficient to maintain Stephens, Luby, and their small staff at little above starvation standard. Yet still the work went on and the numbers grew, largely, as far as I could ever gather, owing to local expenditure, both of time and money, but most of the first, for during all these years and during those to come, our young men spent most of their Sundays and other leisure time in spreading the light that was in them. By the time then at which I have now arrived, the organization may be said to have spread over Leinster and Munster, to be fast gaining ground in Connaught, and to have made a fair start in Ulster.

And here I must somewhat repeat what I said before, in a different connection, about these two provinces, in order that I may say some little more about the two men who were our most active propagandists in these regions. I said before, apropos of I know not what, that I gathered from various sources that it was easier, at nearly all times, but certainly during the earlier stages of our organization, to turn an Orangeman into a Fenian than to effect the same metamorphosis with a Ribbonman. Still at this time we were largely impressing ourselves upon Connaught, and Connaught was (as, indeed, I fear it still is) the headquarters of Ribbonism. I said before, too, that our success in Connaught was largely due to Edward Duffy, in whom an all-absorbing and overpowering fervour of devotion to the cause seems to have more than made up for the absence of any special knowledge or even, as far as I could see, of any mental capacity above the ordinary. Duffy I saw frequently during this *Irish People* time, and to see him was to like him; and I now regret that I did not see him oftener and come to know him better. My opinion of him, though, of course, necessarily based on my own knowledge, is to a large extent influenced by that of others, notably of my sister, who knew him much better than I did, and had a higher opinion of his capacity.

But it matters very little how much or how little of a sage he was; he was certainly very much of a saint, and altogether a martyr.[1]

Of John Nolan, who was mainly instrumental in spreading the organization in the North, I personally knew less than I did of Duffy, though indirectly I heard and even knew a good deal about him, among other ways hearing from him constantly in the paper. Judging him from his work, which is the best test of most men, he must have had more than ordinary capacity in many ways, and most certainly he had more than ordinary activity and energy. There is no halo around his memory as there is around Duffy's, but not the less was he a good man and true, doing in his day good work for Ireland, and so deserving at the least such slight record of himself and his services as they get here.[2]

[1] Two things lend a somewhat adventitious importance to Duffy and his memory; the first was his appointment by Stephens, why I scarcely know, as a sort of head of the organization during his own absence; the second was his sad and almost inevitable death in prison. In neither of these cases was there any special merit, though in what led up to them there necessarily was. He could not help dying in prison, but he could easily have avoided going there at all, and Ireland never forgets those who die for her, though she often forgets and neglects those who merely live for her.

[2] John Nolan (whom I must caution the reader against confounding with another John Nolan, of Amnesty fame) died, I understand, not many years after the time of which I am now writing. Here, too, I may at least mention the name of Andrew Nolan, the brother of John, who then and long before was one of our most energetic workers, but the seat of his activity was Leinster, not Ulster. They were both, I believe, Carlow men by birth and family, and both, I think, commercial travellers by profession.

CHAPTER VI.

THE PAPER AGAIN—MISS FANNY PARNELL—KICKHAM AND THE ARCHBISHOP OF TORONTO.

BUT to come back to the scene and the subject of my chief labours at this time. I have indeed been talking for a good while nearly altogether about the chief writers for the paper, but not as writers. I must now take them up again in this last capacity, or rather deal with what they said, and why they said it. Of course I can only treat this subject very imperfectly, being necessarily obliged to give the *ipsissima verba* but sparingly, lest I should swell this volume out of all fair proportions. Yet still I am painfully conscious that without the words, and a great many of them, no adequate conception of the situation can be formed by the reader. I could have wished that some "Voice of the Irish People" had already made itself heard by the people, and I am not altogether without hope that sometime or other it may; meantime, I can only go on with my narrative, which will lead me, more or less methodically, if cursorily, through the pages of that paper.

I scarcely know at what number of the *People* I came

to a halt, but I take it up again at its twenty-sixth number, after an existence of exactly six months. In this number I find for the first time the name, or rather *nom de plume*, of one who became well known to our readers afterwards, and very much better known since to a very much bigger audience here and in America; I allude to Miss Fanny Parnell and her first contribution, called "Masada" and signed "Aleria." These verses, like all I have seen from that lady's hand, are, I think, rather rhetoric than poetry, though very vigorous and sonorous rhetoric indeed, giving great promise for a girl, as the writer then was. I give the first four lines of the poem and the four that conclude it, for the curious in such things:

Wild and haggard stood the warrior, worn with watching and with pain;
Many a dent was on his breast-plate, on his sword was many a stain;
Loose back o'er his mailed shoulders streamed the tangled locks of coal,
Fiercely from his black eyes flamed all the tempest in his soul.

* * * * * *

Such Masada's mournful story in the bloody days of old,
When the hearts in Hebrew bosoms for their fatherland were bold.
Rest in peace, ye dauntless heroes—rest ye in your gory grave,
God hath seen and God hath heard you; God will soon arrive to save.

It is needless to say more of the story told in the intervening lines than that it was one of men, who, at the call of their leader, first slew their wives and children, and then themselves rather than yield themselves prisoners and consequently slaves. The moral was, of course, everything we could desire, though the example is one that can scarcely be followed in later times, when conquest involves moral rather than material enslavement.

In the same number of the paper a most valuable letter of the Bishop of Toronto—as valuable indeed almost to-day as then—was reprinted and made the text of a long article by Kickham, in which by extract and comment he "points a moral" for the bishops and priests of Ireland. "The state of things," says Kickham, "which the bishop lays bare is truly appalling. The world never witnessed anything like the misery and degradation of the outcast children of Erin." He then analyzes some figures given by the Bishop about Canadian gaols, which showed an alarming preponderance of Irishmen, and still more of Irishwomen, over the people of all other nationalities. "The total number of prisoners of both sexes in 1863 in Toronto was 1901. *Of these one thousand one hundred and sixty-eight were Irish, seven hundred and three of the number being Irish women.*" This state of things, which was by no means confined to Canada, afforded a strong commentary upon a supposed saying of Archbishop Cullen's, that the famine of '45 was a dispensation of Providence, to drive the Irish abroad to spread the Catholic faith. They might in a queer sense be spreading the faith, but they were certainly not improving the morals of the peoples among whom they passed. The Bishop gives a very simple, and no doubt true, reason for this relative criminality of the Irish: "The Germans, French, and even the Norwegians come provided with the means of establishing themselves either as farmers or mechanics;

but the large majority of the Irish come absolutely penniless." To show that you can point no racial moral, at least from the statistics of the Canadian gaols, Kickham notices that while English, Scotch, and others, in greater or lesser numbers, were in gaol, no single Frenchman seems to have been imprisoned during that year. Farther on we have an extract from the Bishop which is still very interesting, and I think nearly as instructive as it ever was. "When the Irish come to America and see the freedom the people enjoy, and the laws protecting the poor tenant as well as the rich landlord, and no compulsory support of a state church which they detest, their feelings of exasperation against their former rulers know no bounds; they take the oath of allegiance to the United States almost immediately on their arrival, and renounce their former allegiance with a vengeance. The youth moreover are not so submissive to the counsels of the clergy in politics as in Ireland, as may be inferred from the proceedings at the processions in New York, Buffalo, Chicago, and other places; and hence the principles of Fenianism have spread themselves more or less through the entire country. The members of the Irish associations in the States and in Canada are computed by good authority to number about one million, and all are animated with the one wish—to see the miserable condition of the Irish improved, as they are ashamed of the taunts which the people of other nations indulge in at their expense."

Kickham goes on to say that the above extract is well worth giving, notwithstanding its implied censure, and after all what is the censure (to other than ecclesiastical eyes) but praise, for, as he remarks, "to talk of submission to clergymen in politics would rather astonish the Catholics of any country in the world but Ireland." Yet perhaps in no country in the world have clergymen proved themselves such bad politicians as in Ireland. The Bishop's statement that Fenianism was spreading in America because the Irish there were less obedient to the priesthood Kickham of course accepts, and thus comments on it: "This is quite true. If the people were submissive to the clergy in politics there would be no Fenian brotherhood. Ireland would be allowed to perish without a hand being raised to help her. No candid thinking man will deny this. We saw from the first ecclesiastical authority in temporal affairs should be shivered to atoms before we could advance a single step towards the liberation of our suffering country. Yet shallow fools and designing knaves wonder, or affect to wonder, why we 'attack the priests.' We never uttered a word against the priests as ministers of religion. But we challenged and do challenge their right to dictate to the people in politics." Here we have our doctrine of "no priests in politics" in a manner formulated. It has been called an anti-Catholic doctrine, but why?[1] We did not hold that priests should be excluded from politics, but that as politicians they should be heeded no more than other men, but rather less, as they have mostly shown themselves very bad politicians. We also

[1] I see it so called by an intelligent and apparently liberal-minded priest the very day I am writing.

held, and I hold still, that the more a priest holds aloof from active politics, and confines himself to his spiritual duties, the better it will be for the bodies as well as the souls of the flocks, as indeed for the bodies and souls of the shepherds too. I cannot imagine how this doctrine, or any part of it, can be held to be anti-Catholic, and I am confident it is more Catholic, as I am sure it is more reasonable, than the doctrine lately set forth on high ecclesiastical authority that a man who believes *all* (I suppose there is some peculiar force in the *all*) his bishops and priests have gone wrong in politics had better change his religion.

Kickham follows up by an extract from the Bishop's letter, which is too lengthy to be given here, but a sentence or two I may quote, superadding Kickham's comments. The whole is a horrible account of the physical and moral status of Irish men and women all over the continent of America. "There has been more *Irish* blood spilled," says the bishop, "in the American war than in *Poland* in the struggle for liberty, and more lives lost in swamps, making railroads, digging canals, by steamboat explosions, and from bad whisky—forced upon Irish labourers by taskmasters desirous of exacting the greatest amount of work from them in their excited state—than would make up the population of a considerable state." This seems, though it is certainly not intended, to be a very good argument in favour of the Mitchelite doctrine that men had better fight, with such arms as they could procure, and, if needs be, fall in the fight, than die in a ditch in Ireland or in these American swamps of which the bishop talks.

But the height of the agony is reached in the very simply-worded sentence which closes the extract from the bishop. "We were informed by the acting parish priest of Montreal that *that city was comparatively chaste until the years* 1852-3, *when numerous bands of girls were brought from the poorhouses of Ireland and distributed through the city*." The italics are Kickham's, whose surprise and indignation breaks out after the following fashion. "Oh! Merciful God, has it come to this! Think of it, Irishmen. American cities are *polluted* by your countrywomen. The women of Ireland were famed for their purity all the world over. But see what English laws can do. The Bishop of Toronto thinks that the workhouse system in Ireland must be most degrading and immoral in its tendency. He has given ample proof that English rule in Ireland is immoral and degrading in its tendency. His lordship says that Irishmen in America are ashamed of the taunts that the people of other nations indulge in at their expense, and are animated by the one wish to see tho miserable condition of the Irish people improved. But does not the Bishop of Toronto know that it is our glory to be the martyr nation? It is the mercy of Heaven that Irish men and women are wallowing in crime and misery from Quebec to New Orleans; and that cities are comparatively chaste till Irish work-

[1] Of course I cannot try to improve the bishop's style, which seems faulty enough at times; but the sense is clear enough, and 'tis that which matters all in this case.

house girls corrupt them. Does the Bishop of Toronto know that the defects of the English constitution are like the spots on the sun? Here is something which Doctor Cullen[1] and Doctor Moriarty (at both of whom Kickham had been driving above, by his allusions to the martyr nation and the spots on the sun) would do well to reflect on. A religious persecution would produce martyrs; but the social persecution and oppression of the poor ruin souls." Kickham proceeds to ask the Irish Hierarchy and priesthood whether it is "the principles of Fenianism" which have caused the loss of millions of Catholics to the Church of America, or whether they have made Irishmen "Plug Uglies," or "Blood Tubs," and goes on to answer, with substantial truth, though with some rhetorical excess, "No, my lords and gentlemen, it is your principles have done all this. Reconcile it to your conscience if you can; but, as the Lord liveth, you, the spiritual guides of the Irish people, have been and are one of the chief props of a system the most

[1] At this distance of time, and with a public highly *incuriosa suorum*, it may not be quite unnecessary to say that Dr. Cullen was then Archbishop of Dublin and afterwards a Cardinal, and was then, as always, one of the most dogmatic, domineering, and self-willed of men, with much of what he took to be, and what in a sense was, religion, but with apparently no feeling about his country other than that it was a good Catholic machine, fashioned mainly to spread the faith over the world. Dr. Moriarty, the Bishop of Kerry, was in many respects an abler man than Cullen, but far less strong-willed, which does not mean, however, that he was in any way weak. He was very much less Roman than his brother bishop, but then, *en revanche*, he was the very much worse or, at least less natural, thing, an offensively pronounced and, I suppose, convinced West Briton. He was always the *bête noir* of the Nationalists, though I don't know that he was any worse, that is more un-Irish, than many other bishops before and since.

fruitful of crime and misery that the world has ever seen."

Kickham winds up his article by an extract from the Bishop which is curiously suggestive even at the present day. "Without venturing to suggest any definite plan of operation in Ireland, could we, in America, by a combination of all the societies—nearly one million strong—on the plan followed by O'Connell in his struggles for Emancipation, and which greatly swelled the Catholic Rent Fund, stretch a helping hand across the ocean to our persecuted and impoverished brethren, in the well grounded hope that England, in her wisdom, will see the necessity of doing justice to Ireland, where her cause is backed by such a powerful combination? We know very prosperous Irishmen who have expressed themselves most willing to mortgage half their property to secure permanent relief for Ireland." Kickham says these are "the principles of Fenianism" (but they are certainly not all the principles), and that "the Fenians are pulling some of the bishops after them" (which was false prophecy), and that this bishop certainly threatens England with a powerful combination. He closes by saying, "We shall be curious to see what the pro-British bishops in Ireland will say to this. But it does not matter much what they say."

CHAPTER VII.

EMIGRATION—PRIESTS IN POLITICS.

I HAVE dwelt at all this length upon the Bishop of Toronto's letter, and what Kickham thought of it and its revelations, because they made a great stir at the time, and were made such good use of then and afterwards, by Kickham and others, against our Cullens, Moriartys, and the like. Then, the document is almost as important now as when it was written, teaching very much the same lessons to the men of this day as of that, though perhaps now the blame for the horrible state of things which existed then, and which largely exists still, might be somewhat more evenly distributed. Emigration still goes on, with only intermittently interrupted activity, and, as far as I know, nearly [1] as unregulated as ever, and here comes in the reason for a somewhat new distribution of blame.

[1] Of course we have all heard of the great exertions made by Miss Charlotte O'Brien to see to the better treatment of the female emigrants on the passage, and to protect them when they land, and now we hear of a Father O'Reardon, who, probably owing to the initiative of Miss O'Brien, has organized some sort of society for this latter purpose in New York. All this is of course very well, but I do not know how much of it there is, or how much there is in it, and, anyway, it touches only the fringes of the great question of emigration.

England and English rule are, of course, still at the root of the evil, but while we must, many of us, leave our country, there is not the same necessity why we should leave it under such unfavourable conditions. There should be (and there are not, that I know of) societies both in Ireland and America, to, if possible, supply the emigrants with some funds when they land, but at least to see that most of them are sent on to those Western regions for which they are suited, and not left to rot in the seaboard cities. Where are those well-to-do Irishmen, mentioned by the Bishop of Toronto, who were willing to give away half their fortunes for some indefinite scheme? Why have they never since done anything, or anything worth speaking of, to regulate emigration?

But this subject of emigration, though something I should perhaps say of it in this connection, is too big a one for complete treatment here, and but remotely involved in my recollections. One side of the subject is, however, vitally connected with them. Irishmen still, thank God, leave their country with the hatred of England lying deep in their souls. For them there is no pretence of union of hearts, nor of anything but war with England, for which they are at all times willing to supply the sinews. But these are not generally the well-to-do, but, unfortunately, the too often ill-to-do, and, sometimes, alas! even the ill-doing. But let us hope that many sins and shortcomings may be forgiven them for the one virtue which they undoubtedly possess to perfection. These Irish in America, and elsewhere out of Ireland, whom the *Times* so long ago gloated over as "gone with a vengeance," are still the strong hope and the sure help of the Irish at home. In the old Fenian times, from which I am trying to gather together these recollections, the Irish abroad were willing to give us their bodies as well as their purses; now we only ask from them the last, and these they are ever ready to give, when appealed to for any adequate cause, or sometimes even on any plausible pretext.

I scarcely know why I go on with this rambling talk about Irishmen abroad, save that I have so long been an Irishman abroad myself that the subject has a charm for me.

History is for ever repeating itself, and often with astonishing closeness. I find myself, for instance, reading in my morning paper, and from the pen of a priest too, opinions and sentiments bearing the closest resemblance to much which I find in an article by Kickham, headed "Priests and Politics," in our twenty-eighth number. "There are men in Ireland at present, who, while representing themselves as Nationalists, seem to regard it as a fundamental principle in politics, that it is unlawful to embark in any project of National regeneration without first consulting the oracles of the Catholic Church and asking for their sanction. Against this notion we deem it our duty strongly to protest. We regard it as a notion at once delusive and pernicious." He goes on to allow fully, what it is only assumed that any man in his senses denies, that religion and morality are constantly mixed up with politics, as they are indeed with nearly everything else, but often almost inextricably, and that in any case priests are no fitter, but rather more unfit, to untie political knots than other men. Here is a passage which might have been written to-day, and something like which is sure to be written to-morrow: "We may safely affirm that, as a general rule, ecclesiastics are not to be coveted as political guides. It is natural we should expect to find in them a knowledge of all essential truths of theology. But it is ludicrously illogical to infer that, because they are acquainted with theology, they must necessarily be political adepts. 'Twould be as sensible to conclude that a good doctor couldn't scribble doggerel. So far from priests being infallible in politics, they are, generally speaking, the most unsafe and fallible of all political teachers. This truth has been illustrated over and over again in Irish affairs. Their electioneering blunderings and divisions have shocked all persons possessed of unprejudiced minds." Then we have particular examples of the fallibility of priestly politicians, with the inevitable names of Sadlier and Keogh trotted out to point the moral. These names were familiar as household words at that time, but have nearly faded out of men's memory since, till recent events, suggesting parallels which time alone can prove either true or false, revived the public interest in these erewhile pets of the priests. I give the passages from Kickham as another example, in a short compass, of that teaching of ours which was nicknamed "No priests in politics." We did not want to force priests out of politics, but only wished their own sense would keep them out, and, when it didn't, we advised that they should be met, on the part of the people, with that entire want of confidence to which their errors of judgment, to mention no worse faults, had alone entitled them.

Such were our views some thirty years ago. They are my views still, only very much strengthened by the events of recent Irish history. We have had priests in politics again with a vengeance, in the Land League and the National League, and how they have spoken and acted for the last dozen years or so it must be for some future historian to pronounce. It is not for me to say in these pages what I think of the later developments of the Irish ecclesiastical spirit, but I suppose priests can scarcely (theoretically at least) object to my sharing the views of the Head of their own Church in the matter of Boycotting and the like. Indeed, I have been one of the very few Nationalists who have anticipated the views of his Holiness, with the result of being as much (or as little) heeded as he.

CHAPTER VIII.

THE STRONG FARMERS—THE ORGANIZATION.

I HAVE let Kickham speak mostly up to this upon "priests in politics," and I shall have to let him speak on the same subject again, but he had many more than one string to his bow, and, like all of us, shot at all sorts of enemies, or knock-kneed friends of the National cause. A little I may give here, and I am sorry I cannot give the whole article, of what he had to say on the peculiar pets of the present (or, perhaps I should rather say, the late) agitation. If there was ever a man with the profoundest sympathy with the agricultural classes generally, and whose whole surroundings and relations were calculated to prejudice him in favour of farmers, and even strong farmers, it was Kickham. And yet this is how he speaks of the class of people whom he calls "graziers" in the thirty-sixth number of the paper. "There is a class of Irishmen of whom we have never spoken—except incidentally—either in praise or blame. We mean the large farmers. . . . Yet we think it well to let those large farmers know that we are not ignorant of their existence. There are some good men amongst them; but, as a class, those men of bullocks are about the worst men in Ireland.

They appear to have no more souls than the brutes which they fatten for the tables of our English masters. So long as they are allowed to possess a certain number of acres—for which they pay dearly—they care not what becomes of Ireland. They have no sympathy for the people. They see woe, and poverty, and hunger all around them, but the sight does not affect them. They see the people melting away—driven like wild beasts from the land of their birth and their love—but they care not. They look upon the mountains and the rivers, and all the wealth and loveliness of our green land, without a throb of pride or sorrow, without one patriot wish, one manly aspiration. Those large farmers are but pampered slaves. They are looked down upon even by the smallest of the small gentry, or at best condescendingly recognized on the fair green, or in the stable. They have much of the arrogant assumption of 'gentility' without any of its refinement. For very many of them are but boors in broadcloth." I cannot give the greater part of the article, but it goes on to appeal to the sons of the farmers, on patriotic and prudential grounds. "A little reflection would enable them to see, even from a selfish point of view, that their fathers cannot easily provide big farms for all of them. They would[1] see, too, that if the people be swept away there will be no patients, clients, or customers for doctors,

[1] What is much more visible now than when Kickham wrote. There are, for instance, I am told, some 400 barristers, for about forty of whom only is there business, and of doctors without patients, or shopkeepers without customers, hard would it be, I fancy, to estimate the numbers.

lawyers, or traders." The article winds up with an appeal to the better feelings of all Irishmen, even including strong farmers. "Yet God knows how anxious we are to lessen the number of Irish-born men who must be treated as foes to their country. We have all confidence in the forbearance and generosity of the Irish people; but forbearance and generosity have their limits. Next to helping to prepare the people for the last glorious effort to strike the rusted chain from the limbs of our bleeding Motherland, there is no labour which we would more heartily enter upon than that of removing in time whatever may cause bitterness and heartburnings between men of Irish birth. In this spirit we address these words to the large farmers. We trust they will take them to heart."

The reader may perhaps naturally begin to inquire here what steps we were taking to strike off that rusty chain of which Kickham somewhat rhetorically speaks. Well, we were taking many steps; if vain ones as regards our ultimate aim and goal, that shortcoming they shared with all the exertions of all the generations that have gone before us, of that one which has come after us, and, for aught I know, they may share it with many a generation still in the womb of time. Meantime the organization was spreading North, South, East, and West, with all its accompanying conditions. Much drilling was going on, with what practical military result is not within the range of my recollections. But what I do remember is that, contrary to the general notion that these things cannot go on without the knowledge of the police, they did in fact mostly go on quite without their knowledge, such punishments as were occasionally inflicted on some young men being rather for public marching than for secret learning to march, or otherwise manage the human body. Of arming, then or after till the collapse of the movement, there was little, for Stephens, rightly or wrongly, was opposed to the plan of trying to conceal arms. But more about all these things hereafter.

Shortly after the starting of the paper, when from week to week we were hard set to meet our weekly engagements (which, indeed, we did mostly from private resources of my own or of Rossa's), Stephens went to America again, this time, as before, mainly in search of the sinews of war.[1] He remained away some months, and returned fairly furnished with funds, leaving things behind him practically in so satisfactory a financial position that we were little hampered through the want of money henceforward, though Stephens

America, if more than once a strong help and steady encouragement, in this matter of money, to us here at home, may at any time, by tightening her purse strings, as she is, indeed, threatening to do just now, easily become a source of weakness too. Then in the perennial fight with England, so much richer as well as stronger than we are, so much depends upon the use to which you put your money. Swords, rifles, and all other instruments of regular war, have quite gone out of fashion of late, but, Plan of Campaign for Plan of Campaign, is it so certain that the old one was, even in its immediate results, any more ineffective than the new one. You have no pitched battles in either case, but in the one case you put some spirit into your combatants, while in the other, in the case of defeat, you necessarily take it out of them. Then as to the bodies of the men, the soldiers grow thin if some of the officers wax fat. But, then, I am so much behind (or before) my time.

then, as ever, did little to husband such money as he got.

But I must return to my account of the contents and progress of the paper, with which I was then far more actively occupied than with any details of the organization; more occupied indeed till paper and organization landed me in Mountjoy, Pentonville, and Portland, where, for many a long day, my thoughts were concerned mainly with more or less melancholy broodings over my own and my country's fate.

CHAPTER IX.

KICKHAM—DR. CULLEN—FATHER COOKE.

IN the thirty-ninth issue of the paper Kickham deals with what he calls "a furlong or two of Pastoral" from Dr. Cullen, who was nearly as long-winded as some of his successors. I quote a passage from the pastoral, which will show clearly that ecclesiastical tactics have not changed since Dr. Cullen's time. Then, as now, if you differ from a priest in politics, you must necessarily be for subverting the faith and corrupting the morals of his congregation. "As publications, hostile to religion and morality, perverting the judgment by the falsest, but not unfrequently the most specious sophistry, while pretending to enlighten it, or influencing the passions by the most dangerous incentives to vice, while affecting to give a faithful picture of life and nature—form one of the most fatal and widely diffused means employed by the demon for the destruction of souls, it will be the imperative duty both of parents and pastors to prevent, so far as their influence extends, the reading and circulation of such pernicious books, novels, romances, several cheap English publications, which appear in weekly numbers, *and some newspapers lately established in Ireland, which, whilst pretending to be the organs of the Irish people, seem to have no other object but to vilify the Catholic Church, and to withdraw our people from its pale*—all such publications offending against faith and morals, are calculated to do the greatest mischief, and ought to be cautiously avoided and severely condemned by all good Christians. The only protection against the poissn they contain, is to banish them from every house, and to destroy them when they fall into your hands." I need scarcely say that the italics are mine, not the Archbishop's. But let us now listen to Kickham. After defying the Archbishop to "produce one ungarbled passage in support of his assertion," he proceeds to carry the war into the enemy's camp. "If faith and morals have been subverted in his diocese, let him charge it to his own imprudence, or attribute it to his own neglect. The doctrines which subverted the faith or debauched the morals of his flock were not taught in the columns of the *Irish People.* What we have taught, and what we shall continue to teach, is, that Dr. Cullen or any other ecclesiastic is not to be followed as a guide in political matters." Here is the horrible heresy, eere is the perversion of faith and corruption of morals. We declined to consider the Archbishop of Dublin infallible in politics, much less the next parish priest or the first curate. "We have yet to hear," continues the article, "what Dr. Cullen did previous to the establishment of those journals pretending to be the organs of he Irish people to limit the circulation in Ireland of journals really subversive of faith and morals. What steps did h take with reference to Reynolds' publications, *Family Heralds*,[1] *Penny Dispatches*, and other cheap periodicals. We leave *Harlots' Progresses* and horrible suicides to cheap English publications. We have no need of such heroes as those that disgrace these publications, and demoralize their readers. We find *heroes* enough, both lay and clerical, among the traitors to Ireland. Those we have unsparingly condemned. Is it by working on the extravagant fears of the people, and putting forth a farrago of folly and misrepresentation: defending one slander by another, that Dr. Cullen expects to crush the cause of Ireland? Appeals to people's feelings and prejudices are the last resort of a man who finds arguments fail him. Dr. Cullen knows that, though the *Irish People* should find no difficulty in refuting his statement, the poison of his pastoral is diffused through a thousand channels through which the refutation can never enter." This is strong language, but reading it calmly now, some twenty-eight years after it was written, I cannot feel that it was too strong for the circumstances or the occasion.

In the concluding paragraph of the article, Kickham puts the case, as between us and Archbishop Cullen and the clergy generally, in a plain and naked form. "In the quaint language of former times, 'no wood comes amiss to make arrows for our destruction.' To crush the

[1] I fear Kickham did the *Family Herald* some injustice in putting it in such bad company. He probably did not read it, nor do I, but from such little of it as I have seen, and from what I hear, it is a sufficiently harmless, if not particularly lively publication.

Irish People no means are unjust or ungentlemanly. In several instances the clergy have used intimidation [1] with our agents, where they found argument fail them. When have the clergy been known to do this, or where, with regard to English cheap literature? None of those English publications are so described in the last pastoral of Dr. Cullen as to point them out to the public. They are merely used as a pretext, while the most stupid of his flock must see that he meant the *Irish People*, by 'some newspapers lately established in Ireland, which, while pretending to be the organs of the Irish people.' So Dr. Cullen knows in his heart that his policy is hostile to the liberty of Ireland. He knows that plain statements setting that policy before the public in its true light must carry the conviction to the heart of every Irishman, that Dr. Cullen may be the friend of religion, but that he is the deadly foe of *Irish Liberty*."

'Tis hard to know what is in the heart of any one. Cardinal Cullen and Charles Kickham have long since gone where what we think of them matters probably little to them. *There* their motives and actions will be weighed and judged unerringly, whereas our judgment must be of necessity most fallible. But how stands it here below with the memories of the cardinal and the convict? Dr. Cullen's name is seldom mentioned, or, when mentioned, is generally associated with the

[1] The paper, week after week, was crowded with letters, describing all sorts of misrepresentations of us and intimidation of our readers by priests in all parts of the country. But I shall have to deal with this matter, as with the general matter of our correspondence, farther on.

infamous ones of Sadlier and Koogh, while the man himself, with his strong will and, I believe, undoubted piety, is little respected, save within a very limited region, and not particularly loved or liked in any. The name of Charles Kickham, on the contrary, though perhaps less known to his countrymen than it ought to be, is never mentioned save with respect and love, a respect and love which will, I think, go on increasing as the ages go by, and the thoughts and feelings and passions and prejudices of the present pass away. Even as regards religion, which is ever the burthen of the song of all these bishops and priests, I doubt whether any candid priest or layman could say now that Cardinal Cullen was a better Catholic than Charles Kickham, and those who would consider him a better Christian must, I think, have very different notions of Christianity from what its founder had.

But to come back to our story, and the year '64 and the forty-fourth number of the paper, where we find a long article, by Kickham, entitled "Pulpit Denunciation —Priests in Politics." The text for Kickham's sermon was supplied this time by a certain Rev. Mr. Cooke, of the order of Mary Immaculate, who, from what I have heard, I believe to have been a very holy man, and a clever one too, but neither his holiness nor his cleverness prevented him from saying the most foolish thing that had been yet said by any of our clerical adversaries. This reverend gentleman declared from the pulpit that it was a mortal sin to read the *Irish People*. Of course Kickham had no difficulty with the Rev. Mr. Cooke, and little quarrel with him. The mere mention of what he said was enough for all men not idiots. But Kickham went on to show where our sin lay, and how it was "mortal" in the literal, not the theological sense. We meant to kill clerical dictation, and we did kill it. If it has come to life again in another generation, the fault is not ours.

The article, while allowing that many priests were good Nationalists, dwells at length on the utter unfitness of priests as political leaders for the one reason, if for no other, that they were not free agents. "If we knew a priest whom nature had marked as a leader of men, ready and willing to take his stand at the head of the people, we should ask him to pause. We should dread the consequence. Every priest believes he is bound to bow humbly to the decrees of his ecclesiastical superiors. And the censure might come at some critical moment when the eyes of the people would be turned to him,[1] and then the people should be left distracted, bewildered, and disheartened. This is why we think it our duty to teach the people not to hope or wish for ecclesiastical leadership; and we wonder every national priest in Ireland does not do the same."

As usual, Kickham utilizes the Tenant Right movement to show the uselessness or worse of "priests in politics." "Well might one of the best and ablest priests of the League, on finding his effort to save the people

[1] This was what did happen in the case of Father Kenyon in '48, and still more recently, and easily within the memory of many of Kickham's readers, in the case of several of the Tenant Right priests.

from extermination baffled by members of his own order, exclaim—'Tis not the people who are rotten. 'Tis the priests are rotten, aye and the bishops are rotten!" Such was the lesson the collapse of the Tenant Right movement taught one of its prominent clerical supporters. What wonder if the Fenians learned the same lesson, and many other lessons too.

CHAPTER X.

LUBY, MYSELF, KICKHAM, AND OTHERS.

I HAVE dwelt with undue insistence perhaps, and certainly at greater length than I could like, upon Kickham's controversy with the priests, nor have I done with it yet. But Kickham was not the paper, nor, as many people might consider, the major part of it, though, as I have said before, I incline to think he was, if not absolutely the best of us, at least the best for mere temporary newspaper purposes. And how temporary most things are in the case of newspapers is well exemplified in the fate and fortunes of the *Irish People*. How few of the men now living have ever read it, and how much fewer still the number who, desiring now to read it, can at all come across it.

But whatever absolute or relative part Kickham took in the paper, Luby's part and my own was, if not larger or as large, certainly very large, and some attention I must give to something of what we two said from time to time. The matter is not easy however. We should be all read wholesale and not piecemeal ; that is, whole articles should be read and not bits of them, to give any adequate notion of our merits or demerits. I have been led into this vein of thought by coming, in the course of my searchings through the pages of the paper, upon the forty-fifth number, which is about midway in our career. Here I find, as was often the case, the whole leading matter written by Luby, Kickham, and myself, and so I take the opportunity of giving the reader some specimen of all three of us, for comparison or contrast, as he likes, but anyway for comprehension.

The first article, by Luby, called "Doubters and Shams," was, as was usual with him, more or less on general national principles, with particular personal applications, not always too easy for a reader of the present day fully to understand. I give the last two paragraphs, as offering, if not perhaps a too favourable example of his style, at least a fair enough one of his general tone of thought. "In short, no man should join the National cause, who is not animated by strong faith and fully prepared to brave all hazards. Let us have no tea-table revolutionists, who join a cause while danger is remote, who love at once to frighten and fascinate weak girls by tall talk, but who sing small when danger drops on them. He who joins in a national struggle incurs the most serious responsibility. It is a terrible thing to trifle with your country's welfare and to sport with men's lives. The conduct of cowards, who join a movement to gratify their petty vanity, and then, in the day of danger, shrink into concealment, tends to lead brave men to destruction, by giving them false notions of the support they may reckon on in a bold enterprise. The blood of the brave, who perish so deceived, is on the head of the recreants who so deceive them. Wise leaders, however, will be sure to see through the hollow professions of sham patriots and calculate the strength to be relied on in a struggle. Far better it were, in a struggle for freedom, to have but 300 true men, on whom you could rely for support to the last drop of their blood—who, if called upon, would conquer or die with you, like the three hundred unforgotten heroes who perished with Leonidas at Thermopylae ; better a thousand times such a small band than 50,000 doubters or shams." It is no part of my present business to defend Luby's doctrines. Fighting, or any talk about fighting, has gone quite out of fashion in Ireland of late, but I must be excused for still thinking that a people who are not prepared to fight in the last resort rather than remain slaves will never be made free by any sort of Parliamentary legerdemain whatsoever. The second article in the paper, called "Clerical Calumniators," was by Kickham, and dealt with a reverend gentleman who informed his flock that the "principal man" of the *Irish People* held peculiar views on the subject of marriage. This particular clerical calumniator was clearly driving at Stephens, who was supposed to be, and indeed was, an unorthodox person, but who happened to hold ultra-orthodox views on the question of marriage, believing that divorce was under no circumstances justifiable.

The major part of Kickham's article was devoted to a Rev. Mr. Dixon who, at a "Mission" in Clonmel, denounced the Fenians after the usual fashion, promising at the same time to open the eyes of the people of

Clonmel "about these Fenians." "What must be the thought," says Kickham, "in the heart of the young man who burns to strike a blow for his trampled motherland, while he listens to a minister of his religion slandering the men whose lives are devoted to the holy old cause for which our fathers so often bled? Our correspondent saw disgust in many an honest face, during the delivery of the Rev. Mr. Dixon's harangue. No wonder. But does it not occur to the Rev. Mr. Dixon that inspiring disgust is scarcely the right way to do the work of his Master? Unless, indeed, he thinks he has two masters. And it is easy enough to see that he cannot serve God and England!" Yes, it is easy to see this in the abstract, but in the concrete not always quite so easy. Men have seemed, and may seem again, *for a time*, to be serving God and Ireland when they were really only serving themselves and England. Kickham goes on to quote from Father Luke Wadding[1] that "time was when we had wooden chalices and golden priests, but now we have golden chalices and wooden priests." Kickham asks if we have again come round to this state of things, and *that* is a question which, I fear, will have to be asked over and over again.

The last article in the paper, headed "Mr. Hankey on Ireland," was mine. As I have said before, my *rôle* was generally quite different from Luby's or Kickham's. I was mostly critical, whether of our native doubters, shams, and other disagreeable entities, or of foreign

[1] Some readers may need to be told that this was a great Irish ecclesiastic of the seventeenth century.

critics and calumniators. The opening paragraph will serve fairly well as a specimen of the sort of thing I was in the habit of writing. "If we are seldom edified we are almost always sure to be amused by an Englishman's notions about Ireland. Your typical Englishman cannot spend two weeks[1] in Ireland without thinking he has seen everything and knows everything, though, from the nature of things, he can see very little and knows next to nothing at all. As a general rule he knows little about any country but his own, chiefly because he cares little. All knowledge of man or nature, to be worth much, must be based on sympathy; and, if the mind's eye do not look lovingly on the landscape (or the land), there is little chance the bodily eye will find much beauty in it." This Hankey by the way, was a splendid specimen of the *serious* (we are chiefly favoured by the comic) travelling Englishman. He was strong in statistics, and had been a member of a Committee of the House of Commons on Irish taxation. He feels bound then, to tell us, as the result of a journey from Clifden to Cork, that "he could see no evidence in any part which he visited that taxation has any appreciable effect in preventing the cultivation of the land, or arresting the ordinary satisfactory progress of reproductive labour."

[1] "A Fortnight in Ireland" is the title of one of the best known books written about us. Nearly thirty years have passed since I wrote the above, and time has only confirmed what I then thought of our foreign masters and would-be monitors. I have known high-placed Englishmen, even of the sympathetic sort, coming over here, knowing absolutely nothing about us, and going back with the most astoundingly mistaken notions about the state of men and things here.

This is funny enough, but it is nothing to what he has to say about the way the taxes, of which it was complained that "the expenditure by the Government was niggardly," were spent. Hankey "could see no evidence, however, that such was the case. Police or constabulary, paid by Government, and whose wages are necessarily spent on the spot, are to be met with in groups in almost every village." This enlightened Englishman acknowledges that we had one grievance; that was, that we still had a Lord Lieutenant, and that the Queen, or even the Prince of Wales, seldom came among us. Mr. Hankey thought that, if only we were favoured with occasional visits from the Queen, "the whole mass of one of the most impulsive people in the civilized world would be ready to fall down and almost worship her." It seems idle to comment, however briefly, upon such stupid gush as this. It seems an elderly, statistical, dry-as-dust gentleman can at times be as foolishly sentimental as the most silly school-girl. To be sure, this Mr. Hankey was not alone in his craze about his Queen, and what she might do if she looked in upon us poor Irish from time to time. It never occurs to your Hankeys in what a moral position they place their Queen. She will not put herself even a little out in order to link two nations together in amity. If there were even a grain of truth in these bushels of loyalistic chaff, the Queen of England, instead of being the model she is supposed to be, would be a monster she certainly is not. But her Majesty, though she had never, I believe, been even a fortnight in Ireland, knows us far better than her

Hankeys do. I had the felicity, for the first and last time, of seeing her Britannic Majesty on her first visit to this country, in the year 1849, and I can certify that on that occasion she was received with considerable curiosity, and, as far as one could judge, a total absence of all other feelings. She passed down the broadest street in Dublin, or perhaps in Europe, amid a gaping crowd, but, as far as I could at all see or hear, without a single cheer or other sign of sympathetic interest. And her Majesty did not like her position, if one were to judge by her looks, and no wonder either. I saw a very similar scene some twenty years after in Paris, at the reception of the Shah of Persia, who was gazed upon by vast crowds, which made not the slightest pretence of regarding him in any other light than that of a mere curiosity, the big diamond in his hat attracting quite as much attention as its wearer, and, no doubt, a great deal more regard. But the Shah, unlike the other potentate, was apparently sublimely indifferent as to how he was regarded by any such mere *profanum vulgus*. I am perhaps diverging somewhat from Fenianism, but scarcely so far as I seem. Royal visits and lying descriptions of them, and sentimental gush over their possible and impossible effects, may help Britishers and West Britishers to throw dust in each other's eyes, but they most certainly do not make, or tend to make, the "mere Irish," or the Irish "fall down and almost worship," but rather stand up, and scoff or scowl, as their special temperaments or moods at the time being may urge them. I was young when I saw the Queen, and certainly enthusiastic, but enthusiastic about everything she did not represent. And as it was with me then, so presumably, bating perhaps some of the enthusiasm, was it with the vast crowd who gazed on her that day in Sackville Street. I am now old, but if *per impossibili* or *per improbabili*, I were to look upon that Queen again, I cannot imagine that my feelings would be essentially other than what they were then. Times have changed much since, and doubtless I have changed with them. But in some things, and especially in the region of the emotions, I have not changed, or changed but little. My feeling towards England was then quite the reverse of loving, and so is it still; and my feeling towards England's Queen was then, as it is now, one of complete indifference.

CHAPTER XI.

SOME CORRESPONDENTS.

I HAVE spoken, in an earlier part of this book, of our correspondence as a special feature of our paper. At first it was confined almost to some half-dozen men, with more or less of a gift of writing, who treat the usual national themes in the usual manner. But, as the paper went on, our correspondents increased vastly in number, and, in selecting from the mass of materials ever before me, I looked very much more to the matter than the manner. We had always, perhaps, at least half a dozen who were perfectly well able to say their say on most subjects; the others were good, bad, and indifferent in the mere matter of style, though few could properly be considered bad, for they all had something to say, and said it, or were made to say it, simply. I say were made to say it, because, though I never altered save to correct some patent grammatical or other literary blunder, I ruthlessly cut out all merely rhetorical and other extraneous matter.

Out of the vast number of letters, it is not too easy to find the most characteristic passages, which are at the same time short and definite enough for quotation, and it is more than a little wearisome to have to wade through so many of them at this distance of time. I find, however, on the most cursory glance, that the correspondents are in the full tide of battle with the priests, here, there, and everywhere, reporting altar denunciations, threatening of agents, and every other form of priestly intimidation. In the very number of the paper from which I quoted last, I find what I take to be the first letter of a writer signing himself "De l'Abbaye." This gentleman was then, as now, nothing if not Catholic, and this is how he takes up Kickham's theme and handles it: "Does Dr. Cooke (for I believe this is his title) imagine that the Catholics of Dublin, if not of all Ireland, are such dolts as to be swayed by his ravings? I little imagined I'd find the ranting of New England Puritanism rivalled by the Catholic priests of Ireland. Our Catholic ecclesiastical authorities are, indeed, putting the patience of the people to a severe trial. In no other country in the world would Dr. Cullen dare to work out his policy. In no other country, I do not hesitate to say, would Catholics tolerate in their chief Prelate an open enemy to their country. Nor in any other country would Dr. Cooke have presumed to utter his silly, and, I must say, wicked denunciations." After a short paragraph in which "De l'Abbaye" talks of priests teaching different doctrines, meaning no doubt different political and moral doctrines, he goes on to say that "to a Catholic this is a perplexing and frightful state of things. It is time to put an end to it, and I say in God's name, let us end it, as we can and at once, by warning in an unmistakable manner our priests, bishops, etc., that they must cease to play fast and loose with our consciences; and that we are not disposed to allow ourselves and our country to be made the cat's-paw of intriguing legates or any other parties in or out of Ireland; and that, though we glory in and thank God for the faith of our Catholic ancestors, we will not tolerate any trading on our religious belief." "De l'Abbaye" wrote letters in the three succeeding numbers of the paper, two of which were on the same burning question of "priests in politics," and couched in quite as strong (if not stronger) language. And as he was, so were all our other correspondents, save that I cannot know, and do not believe, that they were all as orthodox Catholics as he was, though many, if not most, of them must have been orthodox enough.

I have selected "De l'Abbaye" from amongst our correspondents, as Kickham from amongst the leading article writers, because the priests, if you criticize their public action, invariably raise an outcry of infidelity. They raised it then against the writers in the *Irish People,* but can they raise it now, after an interval of some thirty years, against Charles Kickham or "De l'Abbaye?"

Not that I, of course, at all allow that Catholics alone have the right to criticize the public action of priests. They simply do it at an advantage. Protestants of all sects, and such Irishmen as are neither Catholic nor Protestant, have all an equal right to criticize and condemn any public man, whose words or acts they may deem injurious to the weal of their common country.

Lying newspapers are for ever trying to connect, directly or indirectly, Catholicity and Nationality, or at least what they take to be Nationality. But the claim is too patently false to take root anywhere save in the clerical mind, or in the clerically-minded. Nine-tenths of the leading patriots for the last century have been Protestants, real or nominal, and many, if not most of them, certainly only the last. Who thinks the worse as Irishmen of Tone, Davis, or Mitchel, to come no nearer to our own time, because they were not Christians? The main thing to all of us is, whether a man be Irish or not, and not whether he be Catholic, Protestant, or Pagan. And to take the narrower side of things, our clerics and clerically-minded (when they have minds) ought to see that it is not the Tones, Davises, and Mitchels who make infidels, but rather they themselves and their like.

To come back, just for a little while, to our correspondents. In the forty-ninth and fiftieth numbers of the paper I find about seven and six pages, respectively, of correspondence, and 'tis certainly no exaggeration to say that at least three-fourths of it are devoted, directly or indirectly, to the eternal question of "priests in politics." Mostly the question is about altar denunciations, which were rather monotonous in their theme, though, of course, of very varying degrees of violence in their tone. This form of clerical activity, as far as I could ever gather, was very inefficacious from the beginning. Each sermon probably made half a dozen Fenians for the one it unmade. There was, however, another mode of action which was more or less successful all along. By threatening agents with the loss of business, priests certainly impeded the sale of the paper in many places, and probably suppressed it in some; but of course they could not prevent the paper reaching the locality by post.

Perhaps, before leaving our correspondents, at least for a time, I may as well give one specimen of altar denunciations, which was reported to us by two Clonmel correspondents, in letters appearing in the first number of our second volume. Here is what one Father Burke, a Franciscan friar, is reported to have said: "The *Irish People* he described as a Government organ, employed to put down the priests first and to sell their dupes after for Government gold. He reminded his hearers that any one reading that paper was excommunicated, and that heads of families allowing it into their houses, or those over whom they had control to read it, were damned. As for the Fenians, they were the scruff of the earth—a wretched rabble; he would ask but two peelers to drive one hundred of them before them, like chaff before the wind." I do not, of course, give this as necessarily textually correct, but I have next to no doubt that it is substantially so. It is only one case out of many, and, in all these cases, there seems to have been the one general characteristic, that the priests dealt out hell and damnation to the Fenians about as liberally as the late Mr. Spurgeon did to the general unconverted British public. It would appear, too, as if it were by no means the disloyalty of the Fenians to which this particular priest objected, though that was what most of the priests objected to, for he is reported to have said, on the very same occasion, that "he hoped the day is not far distant when you shall drive the oppressors from our shore." It is, of course, idle to speculate on what this priest meant, as it is idle to think of what any priest may mean, by his political fulminations. His acts are mostly intelligible enough, however it may be with his words, and *they* are always steadily directed to the preservation of his unlawful power. As to words, used on the altar or elsewhere, they would of course matter little, save for the ugly fact that any priest, however bad or mad,[1] is sure to be not only heard but heeded by some part of his audience. The fact that the larger part of the audience, as in nearly all these Fenian cases, hears only to dislike or despise the orating priest, however satisfactory from a political point of view, is very much the reverse from a religious.

[1] I say "bad" or "mad," and may give the case of "New Tipperary" (well known, no doubt, to most of my readers) as an example of the sort of mess made by priests in politics. Here we have a priest, who cannot charitably be supposed to be quite sane, let loose upon an unoffending town, which he seeks (happily not quite successfully) to lay waste, by an Archbishop, whom nobody considers other than perfectly sane.

CHAPTER XII.

A SPECIAL DISPENSATION.

TURNING back just a little I find, in our fifty-first number, an article called "Special Dispensation," and opening with the following quotation from the last published sermon of the Archbishop of Dublin: "Wherever the British flag floats, there will be found divines to lift the standard of the Church. It was a special dispensation of God to disperse the Irish people over every country of the globe."

We have seen how this "dispensation" worked in Canada, on the testimony of the parish priest of Montreal, reported by the Archbishop of Toronto. Still our native bishop continues to think it good we should go "to lift the standard of the Church." Let that only be kept floating, and let us supply the benighted Americans and English with priests in plenty, then it might go with the people as it would. "The standard of the Church and the British flag!" says Kickham, "What a strange conjunction! Many dark deeds have been done in the name of religion. But we know of nothing to compare with this latter-day mode of teaching all nations by offering holocaust to the Devil." This was strong language, but there was plenty of evidence to be found elsewhere than in Canada that it was after all nothing but the simple and stern truth. The article goes on to ask us to "look at these figures furnished by the Catholic Chaplain of the Borough Gaol, Liverpool."

		Protestants.			Catholics.
Males	...	2280	...	...	2783
Females	...	1812	...	...	3083

"Thus," the chaplain adds, "54½ per cent. of the males and 63 per cent. of the females are Catholics, and form a majority of 723 on the total number of commitments."

"These 3083 women were all born in Ireland. And let it be borne in mind that Liverpool is a Protestant town of a Protestant country, yet 3083 Catholic Irish women were sent to this borough gaol in one year, while there were only 1812 of all other religions and countries! This is frightful." "I find," writes Father Nugent, "out of the total number of Catholics (5821) who were committed from September 30, 1863—September 30, 1864, only 16 men and 4 women declared themselves to be in the habit of attending church regularly." "We need make no comment upon this fact," says Kickham, and I may add that there is no need of giving any more of his comments on the other facts. These arithmetical figures, in their naked simplicity, are far more effective than any figures of rhetoric can be.

In the seventh, eighth, and ninth numbers of our second volume I find the paper full of correspondence, as usual, the quantity varying between eight and ten pages, and the quality much of the usual kind. The subject was still mainly the priests, and I notice that in two out of three of these numbers our friend "De l'Abbaye" distinguished himself by the strength of his denunciations of "priests in politics," always, however, taking care to proclaim his unalterable attachment to the tenets of Catholicity. As much religion as possible "De l'Abbaye" was willing to take from the priests, but no politics. He sometimes, however, as many before and after him have done, exaggerated the power of the priests for mischief. In an editorial comment about this time, upon one of his letters, I find myself saying that I did "not agree with 'De l'Abbaye,' that 'the priests are the greatest obstacles to Irish independence.' They are a great obstacle, but the greatest obstacle is, of course, the power of England." This was a mere commonplace, and I give it simply to show that sensible men and good Catholics needed to be reminded that the priests, whatever their intentions might be, were not potentially the worst foes of their country.

CHAPTER XIII.

ANSWERS TO CORRESPONDENTS.

OF course the existence of such a mass of published correspondence at least implied heaps of unpublished ditto, and this involved, after a time, and more or less all along, a good deal of work in the shape of "answers to correspondents." Sometimes, but seldom, such answers had to be private, but mostly they found their way into the special column devoted to them, and nine-tenths of them were, I should say, written by myself. I remembered to have found this department one of the most interesting, if not the most interesting, in the old *Nation*, and I tried, vainly, I suppose, to emulate that journal in that as in other ways. The reasons why most of those answers were written by me were simple. First, it was about the only kind of writing I liked, finding it mostly quite easy to dash off some half-dozen lines of comment, commendation, or whatever it might be, when a column or two of review, leading article, or the like, was always to me very much of a task. Then I necessarily received all the correspondence, and read most of it, and so I was in a manner forced to deal with most of it at once, when I could, sending off the letters with or without comment, (and here I may as well mention that frequent editorial postscripts to letters were rather a "feature" of the paper), to the printers, or noticing them in "answers to correspondents." To be sure, I often gave letters to be dealt with by Luby, Kickham, Mulcahy, or somebody else having special knowledge either of the writer or what he had written, but still the great weight of this burden fell upon my own shoulders, and it was the burden I felt least heavy.

Now that I come to give some specimens of these "answers" to correspondents, I find the task by no means an easy one, and I do not know that the labour I expend will be at all rewarded by the amount of profit or pleasure I may give to stray readers. I have to look very far back, and work steadily on through the paper, wearing out my eyes—eyes, alas! far other than when these things were written—on most excruciatingly small print. But all things must have a beginning as well as an end, and here I give an "answer," from an early number, which will probably even now not be altogether acceptable to an Irish *chauvin*:—

'J. O. D.'—"We disagree with the whole tenor and spirit of your remarks. Not only do we not blame the 'O'Connell Committee' for the choice of a sculptor, but, on the contrary, we entirely approve of the man of their selection. They could not do better. If we are to judge of what Mr. Foley will do for O'Connell by what he has done for Goldsmith, we may hope to have another fine statue given to our city; and that is no small boon to any city, and one little likely to be obtained at the hands of the men you mention. The fact of Mr. Foley's non-residence in Ireland weighs but little with us. Make Ireland free, and your Foleys and Maclises may probably return, and your future Foleys and Maclises will certainly never leave. Until then artists can only remain at imminent peril of starvation. Artists, especially artists in stone, can only find patrons in rich men or in rich bodies of men, and it is rather superfluous to say that Ireland has very few of either. If artists were rich enough to give us their work for nothing, we'd be glad to have them here; but seeing that they're generally poor, and taking human nature as it is, we're content that they should stay away until—"

Here is a short "answer" which gives an excuse for another class, which not only lives on the enemy too, but, alas, too often dies for him as well:—

"'A Red Coat' sends us some verses in which he says:—

> 'There's many a loyal Irish heart
> Beneath an English coat.'

"We have no doubt of it. We know full well that it is too often his poverty and not his will consents, when a poor Irishman takes the Saxon shilling. Our soldier friend is, we are sure, a good patriot, and we do not think the worse of him because we cannot give him a place in the Poet's Corner."

In the same paper, in answer to "A Skibbereen Man," I have a few words to say against a very common Irish prejudice:—

"The name of a man does not make him good or bad, and if you have any disposition to judge a man by this standard, try and get rid of it. We neither know nor care who are the lineal descendants of the above-named wretches (certain informers of '98). Probably they are living around you respectably, fostered by the fosterers of their fathers. Men of like lineage must necessarily be extant in many localities. Let us trust that the race must some time become extinct."

Here is an "answer" quite as much needed by the newspaper correspondent of the present as of the past. We have certainly changed in many ways of late, but I fail to see in what way for the better. I doubt whether the people read more of anything than newspapers, while it is certain that the supply of anything worthy of being called national literature, instead of increasing has diminished. But I fear that in explaining my "answer" I'm in a measure repeating it:—

'Mount Leinster.'—"We entirely agree with you upon the importance of supplying the people with a literature suited to their wants, especially ballads, songs, etc. We do not, however, exactly understand what you mean by saying that they formerly had such a literature, but that it has gone out of use. If you mean ballads and songs written in Irish, you may be right; but, if you allude only to such as were written in English, we cannot at all agree with you. Any of those productions we have ever seen were very poor indeed from a literary point of view. You need not expect publishers to act from motives of patriotism. They are like other tradesmen, and look mostly to their shops, and you may be sure that if they thought they could gain anything by printing national works for the people, they would be most happy to do so. We are afraid the people, for a long time to come, must get their literature mainly from newspapers; and, bad enough, and sad enough, is the literature generally supplied by these. But even the newspaper is beyond the reach of many brave men and true patriots, and what can publishers do for men in this condition? Mr. Corrigan's penny publications are the only things to suit their pockets, and they are generally, though by no means invariably, good."

My readers will remember all about the Prince Albert statue, the use the agitators made of it, and our theoretical and practical objections to their action. The same paper which contains Luby's flaming article and other matter anent the Rotunda meetings has this "answer":—

'A Lover of Liberty.'—"We cannot share your indignation against the Corporation. Good feeling and good taste are the last things we should expect from that quarter, so we are in no way surprised at their readiness to grant a favourable site for the Albert statue. Besides, it matters comparatively little where they set the man up; our great shame being that he should get a statue here at all. Not that we do not think that he was a decent enough kind of man in his way, and we would have little objection that his native Germany or his adopted England should do him honour in prose or verse, on canvas or in stone. It is not more evident that this statue has no business here than that there are many other things which have equally little business, and, until we can clear out some of these, we must be prepared to swallow even worse insults than Albert statues."

I have been refusing all along in this book to recognize any marked improvement of any sort in Ireland of late years, but I must confess that in this one small matter of the Dublin Corporation we have improved. I don't know how it is in the matter of taste, but the feeling is certainly far better than it used to be. Flunkeyism no longer reigns predominant, and that is much. Of course all this neither argues any admiration on my part for Corporations in general or this Dublin one in particular; but all things are comparative, and our Corporation is certainly "more Irish" than it was wont to be, if possibly "less nice."

Of course the greater part of the "answers" was devoted to the rejection, with or without reasons, but, as the reader sees, often with rather lengthy ones, of contributions of very varying merit, roughly speaking, on all sorts of subjects. Here is a kind of collective "answer" to a class of contributors who are a pest to editors of weekly papers, especially national ones; for patriotism seems to take a peculiar delight in the manufacture of bad verse, while those who make a good article in this kind are too often not over patriotic:—

"We have received this week such a pile of verses, that, though very tired, we are tempted to give what we were going to call our poetical contributors a few hints. We confess we do this chiefly to save our own time; for though we are usually told that the authors are hard worked, and only write in the intervals of labour, we are afraid they must have too much time to spare, or rather to waste. Nine-tenths of these effusions are patriotic. They usually commence by addressing 'Green Erin,' or 'Dear Erin,' or 'Poor Erin,' and, after fifteen or sixteen stanzas—in which 'tore' always rhymes to 'gore,' and 'crag' to 'flag,' and 'sheen' to 'green' —we find the poets asking her 'to flock round the flag of her country' or to 'succour her woe-stricken mother,' very odd things to expect Erin to do. Now, we protest against the right of patriots to perpetrate bad verses. 'Liberty' does not rhyme with 'nativity,' and when one line has thirteen short syllables, and the next one fourteen long ones, they usually won't scan. Besides, what is the use of eternally gloating over 'slaves' and 'chains'? Let them write only half the quantity in twice the time; indeed, we'd rather they only wrote quarter, but it would be too unreasonable to expect that."

A little further on there is an "answer," prompted apparently by some verses, but bearing upon other things than versifying:—

'J. S. R.'—"There is neither rhyme nor reason in your verses. Your friend may be a very ardent Irishman, but he is not a very wise man. He should have married the woman he liked, and he would not have made the worse soldier afterwards, if he were sufficiently in earnest. Undoubtedly, marriage has a cooling effect upon the constitutions of many patriots, but these are scarcely the persons who, whether married or single, make revolutions."

I have given some little of what I was in the habit of saying to our versifiers, but some little amusement may be got by giving a few short specimens of their handiwork.

'M. O. M. L.'—"Your verses may be well described by a line borrowed from yourself, as

> 'In language most copious, in rhetoric fine.'

"We give an illustrative verse:—

> 'And though I may wander from Greenland to Gondar,
> And roam through all Europe to Thermopylæ,
> More proud than an earl, I'll cherish my pearl
> In the depths of my bosom, *acushla ma chree.*'"

"'G. M.' tells us he has a long poem, quite at our service, which begins after the following fashion:—

> 'Some time back, not long ago,
> Say two hundred and sixty years or so,
> Sir Hugh O'Neil, a valiant knight,
> Marched towards Armagh with all his might.'

'G. M.' "has probably never heard of the *bourgeois gentilhomme*, who spoke prose all his life without knowing it."

One other quotation, and I shall have done with our versifiers for the present:—

"'A Peep of Day Boy' must excuse us for not giving him in full. We do, however, all we can in the way of specimen. The poet loses no time in coming to the main point.

> 'Arouse ye! Arouse ye! Hibernia's brave sons!
> The old growler suspects ye and won't give you guns;
> Yet some day you'll have Minies and Dalgrens galore,
> And five score thousand Fenians for one struggle more.'

"Our mouth waters at the prospect of the Minies, not to mention the Dalgrens. The poet goes on to apostrophize his country,—

'Shall pilgrims still find you a nation of slaves
As thither they travel to bend o'er the graves—
Sacred graves of O'Connell, Fitzgerald, and Moore?
No! Fenians, brave Fenians, for one struggle more.'

"We confess we did not know that pilgrims prayed before the shrine of Moore. The poet bursts into shouts of sardonic laughter at the prospect of pounding the Saxon into smithereens with big guns.

'Those famed wooden walls of Britannia—ha! ha!
Erin's sons' great intellect levels—huzza!
Mr. Bull, go to grass, for your thriving is o'er,
And we'll cut off your horns in one struggle more.'"

There was nothing anyway annoying in such rhymers as the last, or, indeed, most of those of whom we have given specimens. They unconsciously gave some amusement to ourselves and our readers, and probably did little harm to themselves or to anybody else. But there was another sort from whom we got mostly pure worry and annoyance, unalleviated by any amusement save such as was to be got from occasionally pitching into them. A little more of this "pitching in" I may perhaps as well give here before passing on to other matters —

'Iveagh.'—"If you are determined, as you say, to persevere in your literary efforts, we would recommend you to read the works of good writers carefully. We think you somewhat overrate your ability. We see very little in the verses you have sent us that would lead us to expect much from you as a poet, particularly as you are not a beginner. Writing for English publications, like the one you mention, is all very well, if you are paid. But writing for them, or reading them, is not the best way to learn to write well. The 'historical poem' would not suit us at all. You say you are resolved to persevere. Well, there is magic in endeavour; but remember that merely filling quires of foolscap with rhymes is not the most likely way to attain your object."

"'Un de nos amis' asks for a place 'in a respectable part of our paper'—we suppose at the top of our poetical column. However, we think the most friendly thing we can do for him is to refuse him any place at all, and, in the same spirit of pure friendship, we would advise him to leave off writing verses."

"'G. F.'s' fanciful conceits are sometimes pretty but often preposterous. If he supposes they ought to win him a place among poets, we fear he is much mistaken. He is very wrong in thinking that, because some of our modern poets have been misty and obscure, mistiness is at all characteristic of good poetry. Fine thoughts may be expressed in plain words, as those who certainly possessed 'the vision and the faculty divine,' Shakespeare, Dante, etc., have so often proved."

A good deal of course of the "answers" department was necessarily devoted to giving advice; a very useless sort of thing, as a general rule, but one that is supposed to be a special business of editors of weekly newspapers, or at least of some person or persons on the staff. Here is probably the lengthiest piece of advice I gave in an "answer,' and as much of it is still needed in Ireland, and as I think still on the matters in question very much as I thought then, I do not believe that I am wasting time or paper in telling the present generation what I told their fathers. I know that in repeating this sort of thing at this distance of time I am laying myself open to many more or less just, if not over agreeable, imputations that I am setting an undue value on what I said, that what I said had nothing to do with Fenianism, and, therefore, should form no part of these "recollections." But then I do not profess to make these "recollections" altogether, but only mainly, Fenian, and much (if not most) of what I have given and intend to give from the *Irish People* is not because I set any great store upon it as literature, but simply to show how we felt and thought at the time. *That* at least has some historical importance, if Fenianism has any, as I must necessarily hold it had.

Here, without any further phrase, is the "answer" :—

'Red Hand.'—"It would require that we should write a book to answer your questions properly; and, even if we could do so, it is not certain that we'd do you much good. We shall, however, do our best within a limited space to give you a few hints. And, first we tell you to keep a fast hold of whatever Latin and Greek you have got, and try to get more; for these languages are the only true basis for any high culture. You are not to think you have done foolishly in devoting a good deal of your spare time to poetry and novels. You could scarcely read too much of the first, for there is little temptation even to a boy in bad poetry. You might easily read too many novels—most women do—for most of them are worthless; but this does not militate against the fact that some of the highest efforts of human genius are in the form of prose fictions, and time is not misspent in reading them. But to come to what you want to know about your political education. You say you have lately taken to reading the daily papers and feel the want of preliminary political and historical information. Now we would advise you to read the daily papers only for news; and sparingly even for that. People who read nothing but the newspapers do well, perhaps, to read a good deal of them; but youth is not the time to waste one's self on the ephemeral. To live mainly in the present is essentially an attribute of middle life. We cannot recommend you any writer on Government; Montesquieu is, perhaps, the best, though he is not to be relied on in many things. For general political information read history—not general history, but the history of particular countries, or, still better, of particular periods, for example Michelet's 'France' and Thierry's 'Norman Conquest.' By far the best book to our mind for political information about Ireland is Davis's 'Essays,' which will not only give you much information, political and other, but show you where to find more. You will see from what we have said above that we do not think there is much use in general historians, but to be of any use they must be full, so you will see that it would be impossible to tell you at the same time the most concise and the best, this being one of the few cases in which conciseness and excellence are incompatible. Of books that are at all easily come at, Rollin's is perhaps as good as any other, chiefly because he is not concise.[1] To be sure he lived in a pre-critical period, and gives us a good deal of exploded nonsense, but so do most other writers on the same subject. We have given you a long answer which we hope may be of some use to you, though we are not sanguine about the efficacy of anything we have said, save the recommendation to read Davis. And, by-the-bye, do not neglect his poetry."

I have said that I should probably not write very differently on these matters now, but most surely I should not give even a faint-hearted recommendation to Rollin. There has been so much manufacture of all sorts of history books, special and general, that no doubt Rollin is much more out of date at present than when I wrote. I had then a vague notion that I had got some fine loose reading out of him in my boyhood. There was a great deal in him anyway, though not in the most agreeable form, and how much of him was fact and how much fiction it was impossible for the youthful mind to make out. But then, as food for the said mind, probably the fiction was quite as good as the fact.

Much other advice I gave from time to time, never

[1] If you will have something shorter, we may recommend Heeren's "Manual of Ancient History" (1 vol.) and Professor Smyth's "Lectures on Modern History" (2 vols., Bohn).

again in this wholesale form, but rather fragmentarily, and much of it I have good reason to think was taken, which is not too common a case with the commodity in question. Of course this was mostly not the case with the *genus irritabile.* The poets kept pouring in bad verses up to the last, and were very often, naturally enough, highly indignant at being not only rejected but reproved, or, as they probably considered, unkindly and unjustly attacked. Many, however, even of these were more or less amenable to reason. Many ceased to write, presumably seeing the error of their ways, and some, who commenced with a more or less faulty handling of their tools, learned at last the proper use of them, and so were able to mould into more or less fitting shape the materials at their command.

CHAPTER XIV.

THE ORGANIZATION—OUR RETROSPECT.

In looking over these answers to correspondents, who are all along and with few exceptions nothing if not warlike, my mind naturally reverts to what was all the time going on beneath the surface, and indeed occasionally cropping up above it. The organization was ever spreading, north, south, east and west, but in these later months most notably in the west, greatly owing to the activity and earnestness of Edward Duffy. The West was certainly wide awake at last, but at all points of the compass there was life, and hope, and activity. As to the particular forms this activity was taking, or the particular places where it was most marked, that was directly known to me mainly through these correspondents of whom I have been talking so long, but of course only imperfectly through them, for I was far from encouraging anything like outspokenness on their part. I was very little out of Dublin during the time the *Irish People* lasted, and, on such flying visits as I paid to the south or the west, I did not put myself in the way of hearing much about the practical work. Of course I saw Stephens often, and from him I heard everything that he knew, or at least that he believed, but possibly sometimes only what he wished me to believe. Luby, when he was in town, I saw almost daily, having long talks at least once a week, and learning from him all that was being done or left undone. Luby, as I have mentioned before, unlike Kickham and myself, was in constant communication with the men in Dublin, and indeed elsewhere also, for he made more than one visit to the provinces during this time, and at least one to England. Through Luby then I was mainly, though by no means exclusively, "posted" in the affairs of the organization at the time, and afterwards, through the long years in Portland and during my visits to America, we had ample time to go back over the past, and draw from it such instruction as we could for the future. Unfortunately, here again, unlike Luby, I have forgotten much of what I both saw and heard during all these periods, and much of what I remember is but to me like a dream now. Still much also is clear enough, and one thing is as plain as a pike-staff, and that is that during the time of the paper, but especially when money began to flow in from America, Fenians were being enrolled everywhere, and, wherever existing, always more or less efficiently organized.

But leaving the subterranean element aside for the present, and coming back to the paper, I find, in the last number of our first volume, an article written by me and headed "Our Year," some extracts from which will serve better than anything I could write now to show

how we thought and felt at the time, and what we did, or at least fancied we did.

After saying we came into existence without any preliminary flourish of trumpets—that we had no delusions as to what papers could do—and that we certainly thought they'd do little or nothing if people were not doing something outside of them, I go on to state what I thought we had done:—

"It is no boast, but simply the plain truth, to say that no paper has lived so long and at the same time kept so steadily before the public mind the one great end—National Independence, and the one great means—armed resistance. The old *Nation* meant perhaps the same thing, and worked out its objects with an occasional ability to which we do not lay claim, but there were essential differences which it would be tedious and possibly not instructive to point out here. It was overawed by the great authority of O'Connell, and the mind of Davis could never have fair play in a country which still clung tenaciously to a belief in moral force. But let us give praise where praise is due. The old *Nation* did great things in its day, and, possibly, but for its teaching we would not be here to-day to preach the old creed, with much larger experience and consequently less limitations. In one part of the old *Nation's* policy—its strife with sectarianism—we could not do more than follow in its footsteps, and, by so doing, we have gained the same reward—the hatred of bigots. And here it may not be out of place to use words of Davis on a similar occasion: "We look upon the Protestant's fear of the Catholic, and on the Catholic's fear of the Protestant as rank nonsense. Their mutual dislike is something worse. And yet this trash and this crime have ruined the country. Alas! that it should be almost as necessary to write this [1] to-day as when Davis wrote, and our pseudo-national papers are the main cause that this is the case."

The *United Irishman, Felon,* and other papers, certainly spoke plainly enough—in point of fact too plainly, but never seemed to see the necessity of acting as well as speaking. After a few paragraphs against bothering about such minor issues as Tenant Right or the Abolition of the Church Establishment, and against putting faith in Parliament, I go on to say my own say shortly on that theme upon which I had allowed Kickham to expatiate so largely all along. "Of one part of our labour—perhaps the most arduous of all—which we touched upon incidentally above we must speak more fully here. Our efforts to teach the people the one saving political doctrine have met with opposition at once the sternest and the stealthiest. Several priests, in different parts of the country, have striven with might and main, by public denunciation and private tampering, to crush the *Irish People.* We need not characterize the conduct of our clerical opponents here. We merely chronicle it. The political power of the priesthood rests upon the people's respect for their spiritual functions.

[1] Alas! that it should be more necessary to write it in that to-day, which is now nearly thirty years distant from that other to-day, and now as then the papers are the great sowers of strife between the different classes and creeds of Irishmen.

We have tried to make the people distinguish between the two, and that is our 'mortal sin.' But we have faith in the power of truth. We firmly believe that no threats, either spiritual or temporal, can extinguish thought, and that true speech will force its way into the hearts of the people, no matter what slanders are poured into their ears." The two closing paragraphs of the article deal shortly with other and less important features of the paper. "We have heard that certain members of the well-to-do classes sneer at our correspondence, and scoff at the notion that stone-breakers and pedlars can tell us anything worth hearing. We would ask these persons (but that it would be idle) to reflect that ideas do not go with gigs, and that a man may have a big brain though he wears a bad coat. Not that it is large brains we look for in our correspondents, but sound hearts, which all of them have, though many of them have brains as well."

"On what we have done in the more purely literary part of our paper, in the shape of poem, sketch, or story, we do not care to speak much; though this, we think, we may fairly say, that we have sent forth many things which have gone straight to the hearts of the people, and some few, which, though 'caviare to the general,' have sunk into a stray mind here and there."

CHAPTER XV.

OUR POETICAL CONTRIBUTORS.

I WAS not then, as the reader may see, and I am not now, inclined to exaggerate the literary merits of the paper, but I rather feel, in looking back upon our columns, after such a long interval, and after much reading of many papers since, as if I might make larger claims for literary recognition than I have done above. We have never had a "Voice" nor a "Spirit,"[1] and so to readers of the present generation we are known simply by report. Nor till that "Voice" and "Spirit" appear, as some day I hope they may, can I expect to set matters anyway right. I have quoted largely from the paper, but it has always been with a purely practical object, looking to the *fond* and never to the *forme*, and, besides, up to this, for many reasons, but among them the all-sufficient one of the impossibility of finding space, I have left our literary columns unrepresented by extract, save one solitary one from Miss Fanny Parnell.

I have been forcibly reminded, as I write these pages,

[1] Many readers may need to be told that I am alluding above to two small volumes of extracts, one in prose and one in verse, from the old *Nation*, which had and have (at least one of them) a very wide circulation, the *Voice of the Nation* having gone through certainly some eight, and possibly a dozen editions, while the *Spirit* has gone through at least one hundred and twenty, and possibly through one hundred and fifty.

of my shortcomings, or perhaps rather imperfections, by the death of our largest and perhaps our ablest literary contributor, Thomas Irwin. Irwin, however, is sufficiently well known to the present generation by many a volume of verse, much of which first appeared in our paper. Our next largest literary contributor, and, in the eyes of many, a greater one, Robert Dwyer Joyce, has, though, I think, a younger man than Irwin, gone to join the greater number several years ago. He, though well enough known in Ireland formerly, is probably less known now than Irwin, all his later books having been published in America, and few (if any) of them re-published here. Of him, then, I may perhaps as well give some short specimen, which, however, must necessarily be but a mere brick from the general edifice of his works. Those who are curious to know what he was and what he did must seek him in his volume of "Ballads," and in what may be called the Irish epics, "Deirdre" and "Blanid." Joyce had this one, among, no doubt, other peculiarities, that he was, since Scott, the most objective of English-writing (he would rise in his grave if I were simply, though only in a technical sense, to characterize him as English) poets, and that in an age when subjectivity has increased tenfold, nearly all our verse writers being nothing if not vague, obscure, suggestive, speculative, critical, anything in fact but plain and direct.

Here is a piece of Joyce's work which is, I think, a fair example of his usual manner. He was mostly historical and nearly always warlike. The poem I give reads in parts like a translation from the Irish, emulating, but not equalling, the cursing of Callanan, or rather of the Irish bard he translates.

THE WOOD OF DORREMORE.

Time—the end of the 16th century. Scene—a hut in the forest of Connelloe. The old woman who had witnessed the murder of the great Earl Garrett, relating the event to James FitzThomas, the new Earl, and to Patrick FitzMaurice, Lord of Lixnaw.

My curse light heavy on thee,
Ghastly Wood of Dorremore!
May the dews of Heaven forsake thee,
Never spring rain on thee pour;
May the clouds hang ever o'er thee
A pall of blight and gloom,
And thy best branch never bear a leaf
Till the mighty day of doom.

Within thy traitor fastness
Flowed the great Earl Garrett's blood,
Crying up to Heaven for vengeance
On his murderer's gloomy wood!
Never green grass grow within thee,
Never bird above thee soar,
Never flower thy glades enliven,
Ghastly Wood of Dorremore!

Come hither, James of Desmond,
Thou warrior true and good,
Bring hither, too, yon steel-clad knight
Who roams with thee the wood:
I see the brave FitzMaurice
In his port and eagle eye,
Fit comrades are ye to avenge
Earl Garrett's death, or die.

Come nearer, nearer, gallant knights,
My voice is weak and low,
I—I am she, the aged wife
Who saw the deed of woe,
Who saw the traitors stain their swords
In their mighty chieftain's gore,
In that woeful spot—that place of shame
The Wood of Dorremore.

'Twas on the blustering even
  Of a bleak November day;
I knelt outside my cabin door
  With my last son to pray
For his brave sire and brothers three
  Who fell by Desmond's side;
For Ireland's cause and Desmond's weal
  With their harness on they died.

'Twas then, as from our hearts to heaven
  Uprose our prayer forlorn;
An aged man came down the way
  With garments soiled and torn.
His form like Ballar's blasted oak,
  His steps all faint and slow,
And his matted beard upon his breast
  Like white Benbarna's snow.

But though so changed by want and grief,
  So worn with woe he came;
I knew the Desmond by his look
  And by his giant frame:
The look—the mighty arm that oft
  So well had swayed the sword;
Where the shivered spears gleamed through the dust
  And the great guns blazed and roared.

Ah! he was hunted like a wolf
  Of grey Sliav Suchra's scaurs;
And wild with hunger's pangs was he
  And worn with ceaseless wars.
We took him in, we nursed him well
  Through that long night of woe,
Till the early dawn began to light
  Benbarna's caps of snow.

Alas! that ever rose that dawn
  On Mumha's stricken land,
That my last son was but a child
  And mine a woman's hand;
That Desmond's kerne were far away,
  By Dingle's stormy shore,
When the foe with their wild shout of war
  Burst through our cabin door!

In, in black[1] Dhonal Kelly sprang,
  Base Moriarty came;
A moment quailed they 'neath the glance
  Of the Desmond's eye of flame;
Then up black Dhonal whirled his sword,
  With many a murder dyed,
And the old Earl's arm gashed long and deep
  Fell nerveless by his side!

"Back, traitor, knave!" then cried the Earl,
  "Put back thy caitiff sword,
False Moriarty, sheath thy skian,
  For I am Desmond's lord."
But traitor skian and felon sword
  Cleft his brave heart in twain,
And the great Earl fell groaning down,
  Never to rise again!

They bore his body up the height,
  Then lopped his head away,
And left me but the bloody trunk
  To *caoine* the livelong day;
I washed it from the mountain stream,
  Then raised the funeral cry,
That lonely swelled from my son and me
  Through the wild November sky!

And thus they slew my gallant lord,
  God's curse upon their name,
Be theirs a life of blackest gloom
  And a memory of shame;
They spiked his hoary head above
  The bridge of London Town,
But his body sleeps in holy earth
  Full many a good foot down.

My curse light heavy on thee,
  Thou gloomy, gory wood,
And on the two base felon hearts
  That planned that deed of blood;

---

[1] Dhonal Kelly, once a follower of the Earl of Desmond—at the time of the murder a soldier in the pay of the English Government. Dhonal Moriarty, son of Dhonal, petty chief of Corkaguiney, and dependent of the Desmond. These two almost unexampled villains, after the murder, salted the head of their victim, sent it to London, and were well paid by Elizabeth for their treachery.

Withered, withered, bare and nerveless,
Be their arms and hands of gore,
Like thy lightning-blighted branches,
Ghastly Wood of Dorremore.

It is impossible, of course, to give extracts, however slight, from all or even our chief poets, and it is not easy to select. In the earlier numbers, and indeed more or less all through the paper's course, there were numerous contributions from two writers who had little in common with Irwin or Joyce, and little in common with each other save great simplicity and naturalness. One of these was a national teacher, who wrote for us under the *nom de plume* of "Kilmartin," but whose real name was John Walsh, a county Waterford man, like his more celebrated namesake, Edward Walsh; like him, too, in some of the qualities of his poetry as in his position in life (both being national teachers), but lacking, I think, the force and passion of the elder poet. Edward lived and died poor, neglected, and but little known, but whether John be living or dead I know not, though dead, I fancy, he must be long ago, for since the prison walls closed in on me I have heard nothing, directly or indirectly, about him.[1]

In looking out for something to quote from "Kilmartin" I came across a stanza, from a simple little poem of his, which has a pathetic sort of interest for me, as I hope it may have for the reader, though its purely poetical merit may be but slight.

[1] I heard, quite lately, that John Walsh died many years ago, and that Edward was born in Derry and his parents in Cork, but racially he was, of course, a Southern and Waterford man.

Ah me! but the years they have tarried long,
And many have rolled above me,
Since my boyhood flowed like an Irish song
From the lips of the maid that loved me;
When the pebbly stream stole away the hours,
As I fished by the gliding tide side,
And my life seemed wreathed with summer flowers
And I played by the happy[1] Bride side.
The pebbly strand and the bending banks
Still stretch by the bubbling tide side,
But the time is gone when my heart was young
By the pleasant banks of the Bride side.

Of the fate of the second contributor to whom I have alluded above I am alas! in no doubt. She was my own—my very own—sister. She died some two years ago, and left me behind in a world which is altogether another world to me since. She was everything to me as I was everything to her, and perhaps the sole consolation I have got, or can ever get, from her going first, is that I could bear her loss better than she could bear mine. She had a foretaste of what her suffering might be during the long years of my imprisonment and the still longer ones of my exile. It is another consolation—a slighter one than the last, and not unmingled with pain—that her last years, spent wholly with me, were the happiest of her life. The pain mingled with the consolation comes from the thought that she should leave this life when she enjoyed it most. But I am not writing my sister's life, and can neither write nor think of her yet without horrible heart pangs. I give as a specimen of her work a sonnet, not because it is her most characteristic or best work, which is, I think, to be

[1] Small, picturesque, much meandering stream of Walsh's native Waterford, often mentioned in his poems, and clearly very near and dear to the poet's heart at all times.

found in her ballads of peasant life, but because it gives pathetic expression to that family feeling which was so strong in her,

> But two in all the world who were my own,
>   My very own, the same in blood and heart;
> No time or space could make us feel apart,
>   For we were three in one, to us unknown
> All doubts, all fears; we trusted and we loved,
>   But never dreamed the time would quickly come
> When he, our youngest, dearest, should go home.
>   Alas! how bitter has that parting proved
> To us, not him; he did not care to stay.
>   His was too fine a nature for the strife,
>   The wear and tear, the turmoil of this life.
> Before our eyes he wasted day by day;
>   Yet still, through all, with every feeble breath
> His love gushed out—'twas only hushed by death.

I have spoken before of the death of this brother as the first great sorrow of my life as of my sister's life. Other lives she had afterwards to bewail, in the loss of a half-sister and of a half-brother, strongly if not quite equally beloved. It was an added pang—not to her but to me—that she passed away while a small volume of her poems, which has since met with a very considerable amount of acceptance from the public, was going through the press. I have spoken of my sister hitherto merely in her family relations, but she had of course another side to her nature, or indeed many other sides. She was above all things "kindly Irish of the Irish," sharing in the sorrows, joys, hopes, and possibly prejudices of the people. In matters purely political, all through life up to death, she thought absolutely with me, with perhaps a shade of uncompromisingness greater than mine, and felt ever with me, but probably with a depth if not intensity far greater than mine. She might be said to have been theoretically a Fenian all through, and became a very practical one after my arrest and during my imprisonment, devoting much thought, time, and money which she could ill spare, to the cause. I meant to have spoken of my sister only as a contributor to the paper, and I find 'tis in that capacity I have said least about her, but why I have said what I have said, or how I have said it, or why I refrain from saying other things, is but dimly intelligible to me as I write; now I feel I know but too well, but what I think I know not.

Two other poetical contributors, better known then to the public and perhaps better known still, though, I think, probably not gifted with more poetical feeling or faculty, were Dr. Campion, of Kilkenny, and John Francis O'Donnell,[1] a Tipperary man by birth, but at that time living in London, where he edited a Catholic newspaper. Dr. Campion at first figured in our paper under his old *nom de plume*, "The Kilkenny Man," but, after some two or three contributions, he signed himself "Spes," and wrote under that name up to the end. O'Donnell, who used to call himself "Caviare" in the *Nation* and elsewhere, appeared in our paper mostly as "Monckton West," but occasionally also as "P. Monks." It is not over easy to pick out characteristic or adequate specimens of the writing of either of these gentlemen without looking over the whole of the *Irish People*, and I must

[1] Campion and O'Donnell wrote largely and mostly for the *Nation*, before the appearance of the *Irish People*, but both before and after they also wrote much elsewhere.

confess that I rather shrink from performing that task merely for this purpose, though, necessarily for other purposes, and before I have done with this book, I must go through the paper more than once.[1] An additional difficulty, in the case of "Spes," is that his poems are generally of considerable length. I give one of the shortest, which though not particularly characteristic of the writer, either in subject or handling—he wrote of course mostly on Irish themes, and generally in a very warlike spirit—certainly gives a sufficiently adequate idea of such poetical faculty as he had.

CONSTANS.

When Constans slew his next of kin,
God only saw the hideous sin,
The scene—the hour—the dripping glaive,
The cloven heart—the secret grave!
But when the murderer sought his bed,
And pillowed deep his guilty head,
Beside his couch a figure stood,
And in its hand a vase of blood—
Like a huge ruby o'er its brink,
"Drink, brother, drink! drink, brother, drink!"

---

[1] This is a book of recollections, appreciations, impressions, feelings, opinions, and probably prejudices, but certainly not mainly one of facts, and not at all one of research. I hope I need scarcely say that I state nothing that I do not believe to be absolutely true, but it is far from possible for me to know always that what I say is true. There is no need to quote Bacon and Montaigne here again. Then happily for myself, and probably for the reader, I am not forced to read many books in order to make this one, nor any manuscript, save that of my friend Luby, which, I may tell the aforesaid reader, as I have often, and I regret to say uselessly, told my friend himself, is terribly trying to aged eyes, and hard on the human temper at any age. But we must take most things in this world as we find them, and Luby, if (mechanically) one of the worst of writers, is one of the best of fellows, and one of the cleverest too.

Through the wide world the murderer flew,
To blot the vision from his view,
To every clime, to every sky,
Where man could reach, or think to fly;
A branded Cain, he wildly fled;
But, still beside his midnight bed,
The shadow ever grimly stood,
And in its hand, the vase of blood—
Like a huge ruby o'er its brink,
"Drink, brother, drink! drink, brother, drink!"

Back to his native land again
Has Constans come, across the main,
The mockery of what he was
Before he broke God's holy laws,
And seeks through some resistless spell
The spot where his young victim fell.
Full in the moon, he stood, alone,
His grey locks by the night wind blown;

When from the earth beneath his feet,
Wrapped in his gleaming winding sheet,
The ghastly shape rose silently
Before his staring conscious eye;
"Drink, brother, drink!" He seized the cup,
And to the bright moon raised it up.
"Here's to God's mercy on my soul!"
He knelt, and drained the crimson bowl.

The morning came and the strangers found
A lifeless body on the ground,
And when they dug the loosened clay,
To make a deep grave where it lay,
Beneath a rude unlettered stone
Was found a mouldering skeleton.

I have omitted one stanza here, without, I think, marring the sense or weakening the effect, and so I may perhaps allow myself to quote some few lines from another poem of "Spes," more in his usual manner and on one of his favourite themes.

NINETY-EIGHT.

In the old marble town of Kilkenny
With its abbeys, cathedrals, and halls,

Where the Norman bell rings at nightfall,
And the relics of grey crumbling walls
Show traces of Celt and of Saxon,
In bastions, and towers, and keeps,
And graveyards and tombs tell the living
Where glory or holiness sleeps;
Where the Nuncio brought the Pope's blessing,
And money and weapons to boot,
Whilst Owen was wild to be plucking
The English clan up by the root;
Where regicide Oliver revelled
With his Puritan, ironside horde,
And cut down both marble and monarchy,
Grimly and grave—with the sword.
There in that old town of history,
England in famed Ninety-eight,
Was busy with gallows and yeomen,
Propounding the laws of the state.

I must stop here, though the lines I have given are but the prelude to a pathetic[1] story of Ninety-eight.

I have dwelt rather long on Dr. Campion, because, whatever may be his literary merits or defects, and of these the reader may now in a measure judge for himself—he certainly did us (as I said before) yeoman's service all along, both in prose and verse, and, whatever else he may or may not have been, he was at least always Irish of the Irish. Dr. Campion is, I understand, still living, in the city in which I write, and I can only dismiss him with the closing lines of the old fairy stories—that he may live long and die happy!

[1] This story is that of a mother, who is told by her son's executioners, that his life will be spared if he confesses; but who, heartbroken as she is, still prays her only son to die bravely, true to Ireland and to God. The story is well told by Campion, but I think the best rendering of it is in a poem of the old *Nation*, entitled the "Patriot Mother," and signed "Fionnuala," another signature used by the lady better known as "Eva." The poem is to be found in Hayes' "Ballads of Ireland."

In the case of O'Donnell, as in that of Irwin, there is less need of saying much. He is far better known, and perhaps better deserving to be known, than Campion, and even, I think, than Joyce, though to my mind a far lesser man than this latter. Besides, O'Donnell's poems have quite recently been collected,[1] or rather a very copious (to my mind too copious) selection has been made from them, so that the curious reader is now quite in a condition to know all he will care to know about O'Donnell from this volume and a couple of books published in the poet's lifetime.

I find I cannot now identify many of these poetical contributors, and about several I am somewhat hazy, and, unfortunately, I cannot, as I write, make use of the memory and (probably) voluminous notes of my friend Luby. Some few scraps of verse I, however, pull from the heap, seeking, where possible, that they should be characteristic rather of the political than of

[1] In an introduction to this book, the writer of it makes one of those inaccurate statements so common with numberless people who write about Fenian men and things without knowing much about them. "During the Fenian excitement," it is stated, "he (O'Donnell) represented in London the *Irish People*, the mouthpiece of the Fenians, although he was never a member of the brotherhood." It is probably true that O'Donnell was never a Fenian, but not at all true that he ever in any sense represented the *Irish People* in London. We were, as I have said before, at first represented in London by Denis Holland, ex-editor of the *Irishman*, who, so far as I know, was not a Fenian either, and afterwards by Dr. David Bell, who most certainly was a member of the so-called brotherhood. I have used the qualifying phrase "so far as I know" about Holland, for, after I ceased to be in a condition to know, many people but imperfectly known to me yet did become Fenians.

the poetical side of things, though, of course, not neglecting this last either.

Here are the closing verses of a short ballad, much in the manner of the street ones, which Rossa calls "A Soldier's Tale." After taking his hero from his father's cabin to the poor house, then into the English army; afterwards into the Pope's brigade, and finally into the American army, where he becomes a Fenian, he is at last brought home and made to talk after the following plain, if not poetical, fashion:—

Back in this sinking isle again
  Where vultures drink our blood,
Where friends are scattered, starved and slain,
  I'm told I'm cursed by God.
If I can swear, my live-long days
  To fight from pole to pole,
For any Power, however base
  With safety to my soul;
Then can it be by God's decree
  I'm cursed, denounced and banned.
If I should swear one day to free
  My trampled native land.

Rossa wrote little for us either in prose or verse, but whatever he did write was always plain as a pikestaff.

Someway farther on in the paper, I came across something from Mulcahy, very much in the same spirit as Rossa's verses, but more poetical in form. Neither Rossa nor Mulcahy seems to me to be in the least poets, but the "Jillen Andy" of the former is far better than anything I have seen in verse from the latter. But comparisons are proverbially odious, and comparison here, which is altogether indirect and incomplete, is simply provoked by propinquity in time and place. Here are my friend Mulcahy's verses:—

THE SONG OF THE SCYTHE.

I ply my scythe ere the lark ascends,
  To chant his matin prayer,
And ply and ply 'till the golden rail
  With shrill creak fills the air:
And though I ply and bathe in sweat
  Each "swathe" of ripened grain,
I'm a *spalpeen* still, and shall be till
  We burst the tyrant's chain.

Now, want and woe have drooped me down,
  My work will soon be o'er,
The scythe has wrecked my youthful frame,
  My every joint is sore;
But though stiff and drooped, and full of pain,
  No grass shall o'er me grow,
For I hope yet this scythe to whet
  In mowing Ireland's foe.

There is a third stanza better perhaps than either of those I've given, but the moral of the thing is in the verses above, and I'm not quoting them as any adequate example of the poetical or other gifts of Mulcahy.

I have spoken more than once in these pages of "Mary" of the *Nation* (Miss Ellen Downing, of Cork), how she wrote much for us, but nearly always in a religious strain somewhat out of place in our paper; and, finally, after we had come into more or less fierce antagonism with "priests in politics," she felt constrained to cease contributing altogether. I do not know, and she certainly did not say, that she had any particular fault to find with us, but simply thought her position, on so unecclesiastically-minded a journal, somewhat of a "scandal." I cannot of course give here, what she never gave us, anything in that amorous or warlike spirit which she was fond of in the old '48 days, but there may be no harm in quoting some fanciful lines I have just come across, religious indeed, in the true sense, in spirit, but not of that kind which is generally classed as religious poetry :—

FIREWORKS.

As the rocket, which shoots from the earth to the sky,
Whose blaze is the brightest when ready to die,
Should the life of a poet unswervingly be—
One fearless upspringing from Nature to Thee.

Like the blaze of a rocket consumed by its light
Shooting forth but for others its sparkles so bright,
Should the heart of a poet contentedly live
All bare of the gladness 'tis destined to give.

But the rocket has only to shine and to soar
For one moment of radiance, and then is no more,
While the poet drags onward through wearisome years,
To the sound of his music, the weight of his tears.

Yet chide not, poor minstrel, the sorrows that bring
Their soul-searching music to heart and to string;
But grieving and singing pass on to the shore
Where song is eternal and sorrow no more.

There is certainly no Fenianism here, and it may not be easy for the reader to see how I can associate "Mary" or her verses with my recollections of Fenianism. But the reader must guess. The patriot, as the poet, "drags onward through wearisome years." I hear much around me, as I write—with a sort of warlike sound about it—much about "hill-side men," the "Old Guard," and the like; but all that leaves me quite unmoved, while some very peaceful echoes of that past which was not peaceful stir my soul like the sound of a trumpet.

The name of "Mary" suggests the names of other ladies who contributed to our paper. Of my sister I need say nothing more here than that she wrote for us all along till the bitter end, and that nearly all she wrote for us in verse is included in her recently published volume of poems. Of Miss Fanny Parnell (" Aleria ") neither will the limits of this book allow me to say much more. She too, from the time she first contributed (to our twenty-sixth number) went on writing, at irregular intervals, pretty much up to the close.

Another lady coming in about the time "Mary" left us, and signing herself, first "M. J.," and afterwards "Cliodhna," was a Miss Irwin, of Clonakilty, but, soon after her first contribution, became Mrs. O'Donovan Rossa. She was at this time a young, unfledged country girl, fresh from a convent school, and giving, I then thought, great promise of a future which, I am sorry to say, has never arrived. A small volume of her poems was published some time after our arrests, and she then, and during the greater part of her husband's imprisonment, delivered a series of recitations in Ireland, England and America. These recitations showed, I understand, considerable talent in that line. Mrs. O'Donovan has lived, since his release, with her husband in New York, Philadelphia, and elsewhere, and, as far as I know, has written little or no poetry or anything else. I give a few verses from a song of hers, which are, perhaps, not of her best, but are at least direct and forcible, and lend themselves easily to quotation:—

MY LOVE.

O, but my love is fair to see!
Tall and straight as a bonny ash tree,

And his voice is a voice of love to me,
And his step is of one who would be free—
Free in his sorrowing Erin.
When first he called me "sweetheart" he sighed,
And told me he loved one other beside,
One other who was already his bride;
And I should love her for him—I cried—
Then he told me that other was Erin.

O, but my love is fair to see!
And Erin his fairness is all to thee—
Strong with a lion's strength is he,
And gentle with doveling's gentleness he,
My love and thine, O Erin!

One other lady I must mention whom I have spoken of before in talking of the old *Nation*. This is "Eva," once a Miss Kelly, of Galway, but long since become Mrs. Kevin O'Doherty, and resident at different times in different parts of Australia, Brisbane, Sydney, and possibly elsewhere. "Eva" is not any more than "Mary" particularly connected in my mind with Fenianism, but she is more intimately associated in my memory, probably, than any one now living, with all I have felt and thought and done for Ireland since "boyhood's fire was in my blood," down to that sad present when my blood is growing cold, and all fire has long since gone out of me.

I do not know why it is, but I suppose it was simply from laziness, I did not ask aid from "Eva" till near the close of our undertaking; and indeed I am not sure that I asked at all, and that the gift of a contribution was not a spontaneous act. Any way, it came about a month before the suppression of the paper, and, before there was any time to follow it up, there was a very effective end put to us and our proceedings for the time being. This "chant," for so "Eva" calls her poem, had a very melancholy ring to me even at that time, but 'tis a thousand-fold sadder to me now that there are so many more "dead," and "well-beloved dead," we mourn in common. But here is the

CHANT.

Oh! ye dead—ye well-beloved dead!
  Great souls, fond hearts, that once were linked with mine,
Across the gulf that yawns between us dread
  I fling the longings that invite a sign—
A faint, faint shadow of your darling presence,
  A plaintive echo of your voices low,
Some little gleam, some whispered word that lessens
  The awful silence that the parted know.

Oh! ye dead, ye wild lamented dead!
  Who draw me onward by the links of pain,
To that strange neutral ground o'ershadowed
  Between two worlds, that yet a part remain;
Is there no might in sorrow wildly yearning?
  Is there no magic in the strong "I will"?
In love that ever thrilling, ever burning,
  Keeps lonely watch upon that pathway still?

Oh! ye dead, ye silent, shapeless dead!
  Who will not, cannot force that granite wall,
Behind whose shade impalpable and dread
  Ye hear not, see not, those who madly call,
The heavy sullen air about you brooding
  Will waft no sign or murmur to your ears;
The changeless ebon darkness round you flooding,
  No ray can pierce from those far earthly spheres.

Oh! ye dead, ye well remember'd dead,
  Remember'd so that death can never change
Th' impassion'd thoughts to you that once were wed
  But make them still more strongly towards you range,
Your eyes for me can ne'er look blank or hollow,
  Your touch can chill not, nor your voices awe;
Along that mystic path I fain would follow,
  Drawn thither by a secret spirit law.

But I must have done with our poets. Many writers at

least of good verse we had, and notably a writer calling himself "Conaciensis,"[1] who gave us many thoughtful contributions. Many others there were, whose names I either never knew, or, having once known, have now forgotten. For instance, there is a cheerful and spirited poem, entitled "July" and signed "Mala," immediately following the one I have just quoted from "Eva," but who or what "Mala" was, is to me now a mere mystery. Kickham, I have said, wrote little for us in verse. Twice in all, I think; twice at least I find his signature ("C") in our first volume, but whether he figures in the second is more than I can easily tell, that volume being incomplete and wanting an index. One of these poems, I, on reflection, think it well to give. It is one with a name and a subject which have been frequently used in Ireland, and is the best poem of its kind, I think, with possibly the single exception of Banim's.

SOGGARTH AROON.

Cold is the cheerless hearth,
Soggarth aroon,
Sickness and woe and dearth,
Soggarth aroon,
Sit by it night and day,
Turning our hearts to clay
Till life is scarce left to pray,
Soggarth aroon.

Yet still in our cold heart's core,
Soggarth aroon,
One spot for ever more,
Soggarth aroon,

---

[1] His real name was Mathew F. Hughes, as I learned by a visit from the poor fellow (then in great distress) somewhat over ayear ago, and shortly before his death.

Warm we kept for you,
Warm and leal and true,
For you, and old Ireland too,
Soggarth aroon.

For sickness and famine grim,
Soggarth aroon,
This bright spot ne'er could dim,
Soggarth aroon,
Despair came with deathly chill,
Our last fainting hope to kill,
But the twin love we cherished still,
Soggarth aroon.

Has poor Ireland nothing left,
Soggarth aroon
This last wound her heart has cleft,
Soggarth aroon,
Ah! well may her salt tears flow,
To think—oh! my grief and woe!—
To think 'twas you struck the blow,
Soggarth aroon.

We crouch 'neath the tyrant heel,
Soggarth aroon,
We're mute while his lash we feel,
Soggarth aroon,
And pining in dull despair,
His wrongs we like cowards bear—
But *traitors* we never were,
Soggarth aroon.

And "stags" you would make us now,
Soggarth aroon,
You'd stamp on the bondsman's brow,
Soggarth aroon,
Foul treason's red-burning brand—
Oh! doomed and woe-stricken land!
Where honour and truth are banned,
Soggarth aroon.

To those dark days we now look back,
Soggarth aroon,
When the bloodhound was on your track,
Soggarth aroon,
Then we spurned the tyrant's gold,
The pass then we never sold,
WE ARE STILL WHAT WE WERE OF OLD,
Soggarth aroon.

CHAPTER XVI.

ON THE PRIESTS GENERALLY.

I AM sure I sincerely hope "we are still what we were of old"; but, if we are, it is certainly with a difference. I hear much of greater education, superior enlightenment, and the like, but I see faint (if any) signs of either. I hear little indeed of any higher morality, or, indeed, of any morality at all, and I cannot hold that a slight (or even a great) advance in knowledge of the "three R's" can at all compensate for even a comparative disregard of the Ten Commandments. To be sure, we have the "Soggarth" always amongst us, and as a Soggarth I have little to say against him, or at least little concern with him. He has certainly always a strong desire to enforce the sixth commandment, but I have failed to observe, for the last dozen years or so, any exuberant zeal on his part in behalf of the other nine. But it is no part of my business to criticize the "Soggarth" as a moral or religious teacher. But the "Soggarth" is still, as he was of old, one of the strongest of politicians and—one of the worst; and, alas! the "Soggarth's" singer is no longer among us, to bring home to our hearts and heads, by melodious verse and forcible prose, how the "Soggarth aroon" was one thing, and "the Priest in Politics" quite another

CHARLES J. KICKHAM.

To face page 113, Vol. II.

[illegible] if we cannot have K[illegible] [illegible] faint echoes [illegible] of our [illegible] speaking [illegible] while we [illegible] ever and secured [illegible] which should be drawn [illegible] or satire and mere [illegible] how difficult we found it [illegible] always within [illegible] and laboured constantly [illegible] objectionable [illegible] for the correspon[illegible] thought they might use the s[illegible] the priests as the priests did [illegible] that "it must not be inferred that any [illegible] has descended to the vulgarities which some clerical assailants have not been ashamed to revel [illegible] Here is a description of the Irish Priesthood which [illegible] as I know, is as true of the priests [illegible] present [illegible] it was of those of thirty years past:—

"Everyone who knows the Irish Pri[illegible] that there are many amongst them [illegible] of respect and veneration [illegible] to their spiritual duties, but [illegible] moment they begin to dabble in p[illegible] is easily accounted for. The majority of [illegible] the sons of farmers. They are sent to co[illegible] knowing little or nothing of the w[illegible] from [illegible] they don the coat of the ecclesiastic [illegible] till [illegible]

But if we cannot have Kickham's living voice, we can at least have some faint echoes from his grave. In the second number of our second volume I find a long article on "plain speaking." In this article Kickham points out that, while we always talked plainly to the priests, we ever endeavoured to keep on the safe side of the line which should be drawn between the severest invective or satire and mere scurrility. He goes on to say how difficult we found it to keep our correspondents always within due bounds—how we rejected many letters, and laboured constantly to free such as we printed from anything objectionable in expression. He gives it as an excuse for the correspondents that they naturally thought they might use the same sort of language about the priests as the priests did about them, but he adds that "it must not be inferred that any correspondent of ours has descended to the vulgarities which some of our clerical assailants have not been ashamed to revel in." Here is a description of the Irish Priesthood which, so far as I know, is as true of the priests of the present as it was of those of thirty years past:—

"Everyone who knows the Irish Priesthood is aware that there are many amongst them who would be worthy of respect and veneration if they confined themselves to their spiritual duties, but become contemptible the moment they begin to dabble in politics. This is easily accounted for. The majority of our priests are the sons of farmers. They are sent to college at an early age, knowing little or nothing of the world. From the day they don the coat of the ecclesiastical student till they are ordained, they scarcely give a thought to politics. Pious, moral, full of zeal for religion, and of pride in their order, those young men enter upon their priestly duties. The farmer's son who looked with awe upon the village despot—who put his hand to his hat for the *shoneen*, and was looked down upon even by respectable Catholics—finds himself suddenly metamorphosed into an object of reverence; finds those who looked down upon him ready to court and flatter him. It should be a strong head that this could not turn." And most assuredly the heads of the great body of the priests are anything but strong, and the knowledge acquired during their college career, or indeed mostly through their whole career, of anything save theology is often of the scantiest. Kickham goes on to show how the heads are turned, their owners persuaded they "are brilliant writers and orators," and "then the altar is turned into a platform, and vulgar political tirades are substituted for sermons." The natural result follows; the priests lose the respect of the people, at least of all of them who are not slaves in soul. "If the people," says Kickham, "are driven to speak of them (the priests) in a manner hurtful to the feelings of sensitive Catholics, lay or clerical, let those sensitive people look to the origin of the evil. Let them lay the axe to the root by discountenancing a scandal which would not be tolerated in any other country in the world but Ireland." The article goes on, vainly enough as the event proved, to ask that there should be an end to those scandalous denunciations, as well as to mean tampering with our agents and readers; or, if the few continue these disreputable practices, let not the many act as if they approved of them. But that is how the many continued to act. I cannot remember that a single priest condemned, in his own name, the conduct of his brethren, though many did so anonymously. After talking of the matter of language as being one very much of taste, and saying that if we or our correspondents erred in its use, we did so unwittingly, and were always ready to give a hearing to both sides, the article winds up with a declaration of opinion quite as much needed to be heard in the Ireland of to-day as in that olden time. "We shall continue to tell the people to respect their clergy as ministers of religion; but to insist upon their right to judge and act for themselves in all political matters. We shall also fling back calumny, no matter whence it may come, and continue the wholesome practice of calling men and things by their right names."

I am afraid I have wearied my readers, and shall have to weary them still more, with details of our protracted controversy with the priests. But if I instruct somewhat, I am content, for the nonce at least, to amuse but slightly. Scarcely anyone in Ireland knows anything, save vaguely, of that not distant past of which I am writing, and yet without more or less accurate knowledge of that past, intelligent action in the present is difficult indeed. I go on, then, with as little of the dryasdustian spirit as I can help, to give the reader some notion of the war we waged against the priests some thirty years ago, or, perhaps I should say, of the war the priests waged against us; a war the like of which is being fought over again before my eyes as I write, and which I fear will have to be fought over and over again before Irishmen can possess their souls in peace or their bodies in safety.

In the ninth number of the second volume I find an article, of three columns in length, headed "Priests: Our Agents and our Readers." I cannot be sure that this article was written by Kickham, as I find another in the same paper which certainly is his, but it is certainly in his spirit, and it matters comparatively little whose it is. It is not mine. The article opens by saying that we hear from time to time from priests favourable to our cause, "entreating us to steer clear of the Church and to avoid as much as possible saying anything about the priests." The writer of the article says that that was what we wished to do, and have striven to do, in so far as in us lay." "For the interest of the cause it is necessary that we should steer clear, not only of the Catholic Church, but of every other Church, and that we should leave it to clergymen to teach their flocks the way to happiness in the next world. Our mission is to teach the people how to gain freedom and happiness in this world, and we wished to pursue our course without contest with the ministers of any religion." But it mostly takes two people to avoid a quarrel as well as to make one. We said no word, so far as I know, against any priest till many priests had said many against us. "If we speak more of Catholic clergymen than of any other class of people, it is because Catholic clergymen come more in our way. England's soldiers, her police, her[1] landlords, may be looked upon as the natural enemies of the cause we advocate; but a few hundred priests and a few bishops have taken as hostile a stand against us, up to this, as the worst slaves of the English Government." The article states that we were little affected by the public or private calumnies so loosely and literally showered on ourselves, and goes on to comment on the more material means adopted to injure us. "Priests and employers who persecute agents of the *Irish People*, and who get men discharged from their situations for reading it, are certainly sowing the seeds of evil; and if it produce bitter fruit we cannot be blamed for it. An old adage says, 'They who sow the wind shall reap the whirlwind.'"

The last two columns of the article are taken up with specific examples of the persecutions of agents and others for selling, or promoting the sale of, the paper, contained mostly in letters from the agents themselves. These came from all parts of the compass in Ireland, and even from England and Scotland. It is impossible to give here all the article gives, and not over-easy to select from it. Here is an instance of the *fortiter in re*, without the smallest trace of the *suaviter in modo*. "On last Thursday the Rev. Father ——, Tralee, entered the Tralee Reading Room, and took off the table, at

[1] The writer seems to me somewhat unjust to landlords, but possibly there may be some magic in the qualifying pronoun, and that he means not landlords as landlords, but simply such of them as were on the side of England, and unfortunately too many of them, Lord Edward, Smith O'Brien, and many other brilliant exceptions notwithstanding, have been on that side.

broad noon-day, a copy of the *Irish People*, and denounced every man who read 'the dirty scurrilous rag,' and said that any young man who read the paper or encouraged the sale of it, he would go to their employers and deprive them of their employment, and that any shop-keepers who read the paper he would denounce from the altar, and would not allow either a townsman or a countryman to enter his shop."

It is not easy to know to what extent the terrible pressure brought to bear upon the people to stop selling the paper injured or served that sale. The article would seem to think that on the whole it served it. Here is an instance of another persecution, which the writer of the article finds "amusing," but which I should feel inclined to look upon as simply disgusting. "Miss —— gets the *Irish People*. Father —— heard it, and went to her house and told her that she committed a mortal sin every time she read that paper. She replied she believed she did not, and would continue to read it. 'Then,' says the priest, 'you are a Protestant, and you will not be allowed to the sacraments.' The cry of the priests against their political opponents used to be that they were infidels. This priest preferred the less vague but more ridiculous charge of Protestantism, believing, or pretending to believe, that it was some sort of heresy to differ with him in a purely political matter."

The case of Miss —— and the priest was one of *moral* pressure, but there was plenty of pure material pressure too. I give one case at some length, because it is very definite, and shows a good deal of the working of the machinery against suspected Fenians; the collusion of the priest and the "Peeler," and the like. The priest in later times has been mostly against the "Peeler," even when the peeler has been upholding not only the law of the land but the moral law, but the two potentates are pretty sure to come together again when the question is about rebels, secret societies, and the like; that is, societies whose object it is to free Ireland, and not to defraud your landlord, or ruin or murder your neighbour. But to come to our case:—

"I am a painstaking trader, and was generally employed by the gentlemen of the district. I had the contract for keeping the workhouse in repair too. I used to get the *Irish People*; and amongst the young men who used to call to my house of a Sunday evening to read was one who taught a school in the next parish. The sergeant of police came in one Sunday and he saw us reading the paper. He told the priest of it next day. This priest wrote to the priest in the neighbouring parish where the young man taught, and the young man was dismissed. His sister who taught in the female school was dismissed too. Next Board-day I was talked of by the guardians,[1] and they all agreed not to give me more work, and that I should not get the contract any more. The Catholic Guardians were the worst against me. The man I was at work with told me next day

[1] The fathers of the patriotic Boycotters and Plan of Campaigners of a later day, the fathers, uncles, or brothers of priests, quite willing then as now that England should rule, but then, as still, wanting to get as much as they could out of their landlords, or indeed out of anybody else.

that he'd stop the work for a while. I knew I could get nothing to do at home. I came up to Dublin, and brought my children with me. I would not care only for them." This is only one out of many cases. The dismissal of schoolmasters and schoolmistresses were cases of peculiar hardship, there being but slight chance indeed of any redress by the National Board, which was simply a mere Government Department. As to the petty warfare with our agents which is the burthen of the article, I have said little. The cases are monotonously alike. The priest induces or compels the weak-minded to give up selling the paper, while the strong-minded refuse, mostly no doubt to their temporal disadvantage. One astute gentleman, however, improved on the methods of his fellows. "He was," says the article, "in the confidence of our agent, and advised him to continue selling the paper, but not to sell more than a dozen any week, and to send back one or two occasionally, 'Because,' he used to say, 'if you give it up they'll get another agent who'll sell more.' We did not get another agent, and now there are six dozen sold in the town."

All these modes of warfare were petty, mean, sordid, and nearly utterly ineffective. They failed to put down the paper, and probably did much, by making them known, to spread our principles. More heroic measures, however, were also tried, with little hurt, I think, to us, but with what hurt to those who used them I leave it to the writer of the article to say. "At the hazard of wounding the feelings of some of our readers we fear we must refer to another kind of priest. It is he who in the Confessional gives it as penance to refrain from reading the *Irish People,* and even from entering a shop where it is sold. The priest who acts so does more to bring one of the most solemn sacraments of the Catholic Church into contempt than all the tracts the Priests' Protection Society could issue for a twelvemonth."

The article winds up with a short paragraph upon that collusion, or at least agreement, between priests and peelers to which I have alluded above. "The police are beginning to follow the example long since set them by the priests. From a case we report elsewhere, it would seem that a man will not be allowed to sell whisky because his son sells the *Irish People.*"

CHAPTER XVII.

PREVARICATING PRIESTS AND CONTRADICTORY BISHOPS.

I HAVE spoken of an article, which is certainly by Kickham, in the same paper. It is called "Public Delinquents," in allusion to the use of that phrase by Dr. McHale for the Keoghs, Sadliers, and their surroundings. "Fortunately," says Kickham, "there is one class of public delinquents to whom the Irish people can never show mercy. While one man or woman is left in Ireland, there will be a curse for the *informer*." This is anent the recent case of the burning in effigy of a priest in Skibbereen. This priest was accused, not of giving information himself, but of inducing certain young men to do so. The reverend gentleman, in giving evidence against the effigy burners, swore that he never gave any information, and swore also a great many other things rather beside the question, as sufficiently shown by the following comment by Kickham. "It is easy to see that Father Collins is ashamed of the part he has been obliged to play. But the principal charge against him was *that he induced certain young men to turn informers.* Why is he silent on this point? He gives a reason for visiting the police officer's house. He never spoke to the Rev.

Mr. Freke. But, when he went to the trouble of explaining these trifling circumstances on oath, why was he silent on the *main point?* Did he, or did he not, encourage Irishmen to turn informers? That is the question. If he had remained silent altogether, it might be said that he scorned to reply to his accusers. But having come forward to clear his character publicly on oath, he is bound to reply to the above questions. The people of Skibbereen had good grounds for supposing him guilty. He was publicly thanked by the Orange press for 'leading to the arrest of Kean.' The people waited for a fortnight for his denial of this. There was no denial, and the people took the readiest way to show what they think of priests who could play the detective in the service of England. If Father Collins publicly declares that he said nothing to induce anyone to turn informer, notwithstanding his petty malice towards the men whose liberty he wishes to swear away,[1] we shall be the first to call upon the people of Skibbereen to make reparation for the wrong done him; and we shall do so all the more readily because the *moral* of the effigy will be in no way impaired, whether Father Collins be innocent or guilty. The people had good grounds for believing him guilty, and that is enough. But we may remind Father Collins that he has sworn either too much or too little. A straw will show how the wind blows—and why not a straw effigy?"

I do not believe that we ever had to call upon the

[1] This, of course, refers to the efforts of Father Collins to have the effigy burners punished.

Skibbereeners to ask pardon for calumniating their clergyman, but probably we shall hear more of Father Collins before we have got through the paper and my story.

A little farther on in the paper, apropos of a pastoral of Dr. Cullen on his new association, Kickham touches on a matter bearing but indirectly upon our quarrel with the priests, but having a special interest as showing the methods of priests in other matters, or, as Kickham seemed to think, what tended to be their method in all matters. " He tells his clergy in this Pastoral that parents who send their sons to Trinity College are unworthy of the sacraments of the Church, and ought to be excluded from them! Daniel O'Connell sent his son to Trinity College. It will surprise Irish Catholics to learn that Daniel O'Connell ought to have been excluded from the sacraments of the Church. Trinity College is not worse now than it was when the late Archbishop of Cashel, Dr. Slattery, was a student there. Yet, according to Dr. Cullen, those Catholics who send their sons to Trinity College are unworthy of the sacraments of the Church! Will all Catholic students be now withdrawn from this College? And if not, are their fathers and mothers to be denied the sacraments? We refer to this matter, not because of any interest we feel in this or that university, but in order to let the people see what value ought to be set upon threats of this kind. Even the liberator himself was no better than a 'Fenian' in the eyes of Dr. Cullen. As far as we can see, anything disapproved of by certain ecclesiastics, be it brotherhood, society, school, or college, must be shunned on pain of exclusion from the sacraments." Yes, nearly *anything*, and 'tis hard indeed to guess what thing. In this matter of Trinity College the threat seems to have been a mere *brutum fulmen*, as Kickham points out in the next number of the paper. As regards Trinity, it was said a thing ought to be done, but then it never was done, while to the Brotherhood of St. Patrick and other brotherhoods the sacraments were actually denied. "There was," says Kickham, "no question of 'ought to be' in their case; the decree was launched at once, and backed up in every way, even by a rescript from Rome. It was not said that in this or such like 'dangerous brotherhoods' there was any peril to faith or morals.[1] No one could be pointed out as having left the faith of their fathers through their means. Apparently, it has been otherwise with Trinity College,[2] and yet how different is the course of conduct Irish ecclesiastics think fit to pursue in these two cases. The Archbishop of Cashel said that the Irish people were a shrewd race, and that they were an observant people. They comment upon contrasts such as this, and draw conclusions which

[1] No, but then it is alleged, though why it is not easy to make out, that such brotherhoods are in themselves immoral.

[2] Yes, people formerly gave up their religion, and took on to another, for gain, but people did the same thing for the same reason all over the country. But now that nobody in Trinity has any temptation to deny the faith that is in him, or to pretend to some other he has not got, all the *raison d'être* of opposition to Trinity seems to the unecclesiastical mind quite removed. But then the ecclesiastical mind is different, and is nearly always quite intelligible, if very often far from admirable.

may sometimes be unwarrantable, but to which they are always provoked."

The Irish people are certainly in many senses "shrewd," but they are at the same time very gullible. They have "long memories," but also very short ones. They have the most vivid recollection of Brian Boru, of Dermod MacMurrough, of Murrough of the Burnings, and the like, but they frequently forget all about the day before yesterday. Who now knows much about Cardinal Cullen, or how he upheld the Keoghs, Sadliers, and other nefarious people of his day, and sought, haply in vain, to set his heel upon the Fenians, who, whatever else they may have been, were, in so far as they knew how, ever "true to Ireland and to God?"

But to go on with the article. Kickham, after saying something more about the things which the priests said they "ought" to do, and what they actually did, winds up by asking a few pertinent questions. "Why is a spiritual danger of less pressing importance than a temporal peril; or a rich man's soul than a poor man's body? Would so much be thought of the latter if, instead of being risked against the English power (as supposed), it was quietly starving under it, or flying from it? We confess the reticence in the one case, the haste in the other, strike us as very curious." Well, now, with the added experience of a quarter of a century, these things no longer strike us as "curious." Kickham, poet and man of imagination though he was, saw but imperfectly that to the priest there are sins and sins, many very venial, some few mortal, but one deadly indeed. That you should more or less defraud your landlord, that you should put pressure on or strike terror into your neighbour, or even that you should project pellets of lead into the bodies of presumably objectionable characters—all that is no doubt blamable, but easily enough pardoned; but that you should presume to differ with the Church, that is practically with the next P.P., or C.C., who is but too often the Church in his own estimation—that is a sin for which you probably "ought" to suffer eternal damnation, but for which you certainly will be made to suffer much temporary and temporal inconvenience, in so far as the said priest can have his way. Here, I am, no doubt, projecting the present into the past. But how can I help it? The more things change, as our Gallic neighbours say, the more they remain the same. "Priests in Politics" we have always, and a people who, "shrewd" though they be, are always easily deceivable, and consequently often badly deceived. I have now gone a long way with Kickham in his anti-clerical campaign. I am tired of my task, but still I must go on with it, saddening though it may be, till I come to the end of the paper; which was in a sense and for the time being, the *end* of Kickham and myself, and even, in a still other sense, of the priests too. For the priests remained more or less quiescent for a time, then became more or less active again under the Butt régime, and grew in strength and power as the Parnellite movement progressed, and now are where they are, and what they are all men can see for themselves, and I forbear to say.

CHAPTER XVIII.

QUEEN'S SPEECHES—QUEEN'S LORDS LIEUTENANTS.

IF the priests took up a large space in the paper, and occupied much of the time of its contributors and correspondents, we had of course much other fish to fry, being mostly busy in that anti-Parliamentary and unconstitutional propaganda which the said priests condemned, and which we condemned them for condemning, or rather, far more, for their manner of condemning. An article in this very number of the paper (the twelfth of the second volume) from which I have been just quoting is short enough for bodily inclusion here, and may at least serve to show our attitude towards that great entity, the British Parliament, an attitude which may seem strange to many people just now. We had no faith in the British Parliament, and I still hold that we had no sufficient reason for having any. That sort of *faith* which has since come to many from finding the pressurability of the said Parliament we could not have, and it is no part of my present business to explain, even if I fully understood, the basis of the faith that is in so many in the present, and probably only for the present. But this is a rather long preamble to a very short document.

The article is on the Queen's Speech, and is mine. "We print in our columns this week the speech or message of Her Majesty Queen Victoria. We have little to say about it. It is as meaningless and foolish as British Royal speeches usually are. Indeed every Queen's Speech seems to us like every other Queen's Speech, as one pea is to another. We have only read this Speech cursorily. Yet we are inclined to think that it is characterized by one unvarying feature of British Royal speeches, viz., a certain amount of bad English. Her Majesty says a considerable number of nonsensical things about a great many countries. She gives three or four lines to Ireland. Within that narrow compass she manages twice to say the thing which is not. Of the debate on the address it is scarcely necessary to say anything. Several members spoke sympathetically about Ireland, but all ignorantly. Mr. Vincent Scully seemed to have a sort of idea that things might go on better if he were in the Cabinet. Some enthusiastic Englishman prescribed the Prince of Wales, at which the House laughed, and the House was right. Sir Robert Peel was, as usual, impertinent; but what on earth does it matter what Sir Robert Peel was?"

It certainly mattered nothing what Sir Robert Peel was, save for the cynical Palmerstonian joke of sending such a man to govern us, and it mattered very little what that Parliament was, as it has mattered little what many preceding and successive ones were. The single thing that matters is the *force* we can bring to bear upon that institution, and how much force we can ever bring, or how long we can keep it up, is a problem still needing solution. I have said more than once that, while striving to fix my eyes on the past, I cannot help certain occasional side glances at the present. As I write these lines, we are on the eve of a general election, and I am told that the people are so interested as to what particular bobus or bobissimus they shall inflict upon the British that they can give no thought to the past and but little to the future. I am also [1] told, such strange revolutions are there in the whirligig of time, that I am myself engaged in some mysterious and nefarious schemes bearing upon the Parliamentary game, and no doubt consciously on the interest of those English whom I have all my life loved so well. All this talk about parliament is very much of the nature of an episode, but this book is nothing if not episodical. The scene is for ever shifting, but the theatre of action is for ever the same. We go on struggling against England, but, alas! too often contending among ourselves as to how that struggle should be carried on, and, as a result of our squabbles, sometimes ceasing to struggle at all, and sometimes seeming even to "cave in" [2] altogether.

I have let an interval of several months pass by without touching this book, but necessarily not without thinking of it. The reasons for this neglect of my task

[1] Vide *Freeman's Journal* of June 13th, 1892.

[2] Of course this is only seeming. The leaders, naturally, "cave in" often, but the people never. *Their* great fault, as possibly their greatest misfortune, is, that they but too often fail to recognize rogues or shams till these rogues and shams quite divest themselves of their masques.

were various and complicated, but I need not confide them to the reader here or now. They have but the most distant and indirect bearing upon Fenianism, and 'tis only upon Fenianism, or things relating to it, that I propose to make my revelations. I was telling when I ceased my tale what I thought some thirty years ago about a Queen's Speech. What I (and presumably many others like me) thought of the lady herself was simple enough. I looked upon her as a highly respectable foreign lady, apparently with the merits and demerits of the English *bourgeoise,* but with whom my thoughts or feelings need not concern themselves at all, save in so far as she symbolized that British rule which was so hateful to my soul. As the woman she was indifferent, as the ruler disliked, but scarcely actively, seeing that she reigned rather than ruled, and that she could not well help being English and a Queen, or, rather the English Queen of Ireland. Very similar was my feeling mostly towards the respectable (or disrespectable) Englishman sent to represent her on Cork Hill. During most of the time that Englishman was a very respectable man indeed, well known to us long before as Chief Secretary and Lord Morpeth, when he gave some promise, from an Irish as well as from some other points of view, none of which did he fulfil as Lord Lieutenant or Earl of Carlisle.[1]

[1] I have said before how Thomas Drummond, the greatest Irish Under-Secretary, and probably the greatest non-Irish ruler we have ever had, cast a reflected glory upon his official superiors—Morpeth and Mulgrave—they getting the credit for the time being of what was due to Drummond, and apparently to Drummond alone.

But why bother about Queens or Lord Lieutenants, mostly the mere accident of accidents? Neither this Queen nor this Lord Lieutenant had anything, so far as I know, to do with Fenianism, nor Fenianism with them, so I fear 'tis but another proof of my incurable discursiveness that I have had anything to say to them.

CHAPTER XIX.

HEROIC CAPITALS—PRIESTS HEROIC AND OTHER.

In the next number of the paper (Feb. 18th) there are two articles, the one called "A Heroic Capital," and the other with the heading of "Priests and Politicians." Both articles are long, and it is not easy to give any adequate idea of their contents without being much lengthier than I can at all afford to be at this stage of my narrative.

After dwelling upon the all importance for good or ill to a country of her cities in general and her chief one in particular, Luby goes on to say that "it is plain there is nothing which a country should pray more fervently to possess than a heroic capital. With such a guide and example the nation's thoughts will be lofty and her deeds will be great. Her history will be sublime. On the other hand, if the capital of a country be peopled with men of corrupt and craven souls, the mind and action of the nation at large will, in all probability, be base and cowardly, and her history nothing more than a record of infamy." After citing in illustration of his theme, the names of Paris, Warsaw, Madrid, and Moscow, he comes of course at last to Dublin, putting many questions as to our capital and its attitude towards men and things. "Long ago," he says, "it was a Danish city; afterwards it was a mere city of the Pale; but to-day it is an Irish city and the recognized capital of our race." He might have added that to the city of the Pale succeeded the city of the Ascendency, lasting down to near the time he wrote, but probably he thought these but different names of the same thing, succeeding phases of the same foreign domination. Still there was modification and development; but any way, by this time and still more since, Dublin had grown "Irish of the Irish, neither Saxon nor Italian," and Luby felt strongly inclined to augur for her a high and happy future. Here is his concluding paragraph: "We believe the men of Dublin are true and sound. We believe they will never disgrace the Irish name. In all the struggles of the past century they have had their share. We believe that, when the great day arrives, they will do their duty as valiantly as the men of cities at present more renowned. We trust we shall live to see Dublin brilliant and famous—the worthy capital of a free Ireland! Her situation may not be the best in a military point of view for the capital of an independent country. But, even if a slight drawback exists in this particular, it or worse defects would be neutralized if the actions of her people gave Dublin a title to be called heroic."

The "great day" that was in Luby's thoughts never came for Dublin; physically, she has not been tried, but morally she has, and mostly she has not been found wanting. Nearly thirty years have passed since Luby wrote, and, though he is still living, and I trust likely to live many years to come, I fear me much that he is not likely "to see Dublin brilliant and famous," but I hope he may continue to see her staunch and true.

In the second article Kickham says much in his usual style on the harmful and hateful connection between priests and politics, opening abruptly with a wonderfully appropriate quotation from one of the most celebrated priests of his time. "I arise," said Father Lacordaire, speaking from the bar in his own defence, on the memorable occasion of his first indictment by the Govern ment, "I arise with a remembrance which I could not put away. When the priest formerly arose in the midst of the peoples, something which excited a profound love rose along with him. To-day, accused though I be, I know that my name of priest is mute for my defence, and I am resigned. *The people divested the priest of that ancient love they bore him when the priest divested himself of an august part of his character, when then the man of God ceased to be the man of liberty.*" This was, of course, a splendid text for Kickham, and he had little difficulty in preaching from it. "He, Lacordaire, saw that to a great extent the priests had lost the confidence of the people, and what did he do? Did he rail at the people as infidels, as Garibaldians, as the scum of the earth, as everything in fact which was irredeemably bad? No. He left that to our reverend friends in Ireland, who think they can restore love and confidence by abuse and degrading epithets." The article goes on to show how Lacordaire and his friends acted, how they taught liberty as well as religion, refusing to see any natural antagonism between the two; how he was censured and punished by his ecclesiastical superiors, but succeeded in the long run in, if not winning for the priests the confidence of the people—he could not well do that till the great body of them had become more like himself—at least to a great extent neutralizing their feelings.[1] Farther on, in the same article, Kickham quotes a passage, from another and probably more famous foreign ecclesiastic, still more effective from many points of view, though not from the particular one.[2] "Each nationality," writes a great German Catholic theologian, "has an original *right* (within easily recognizable limits and without interference on the part of any other equally privileged nation) to vindicate and freely develop itself. The suppression of a nationality or of a manifestation of its existence, within its natural and legitimate limits, is a crime against the order decreed by God, and which sooner or later brings its own punishment."

[1] I think I have mentioned before in this book how the priests, in France, were rather popular than the reverse after the revolution of '48. This, if probably largely due to Lacordaire and like-minded men, was also owing to the fact that the Government of Louis Philippe discouraged the action of "Priests in Politics," and so the people began to look upon them again as priests and not as politicians.

[2] I cannot verify this quotation from Döllinger without very much more trouble than I care to take, or than I think is worth taking, but I feel I can rely upon Kickham having good authority for it, for, if no way learned, he was mostly very accurate and careful. Anyway, the words, whether Döllinger's or another's, are profoundly true, and should be taken to heart by all of us, whether lay or clerical.

CHAPTER XX.

DE OMNIBUS REBUS.

I HAVE been talking much, or rather allowing Kickham to talk, all along about the priests. But I speak of them nearly always as politicians, and in that capacity I found them execrable then and have not found them less execrable since. I am reminded here, however, in re-reading a letter from Killeagh, and signed J. McSwiney, C.C., that I was not always quite fair to these gentlemen. But, human nature being what it is, how could I well be? I think, however, having now nearly gone through the whole paper, that I always tried to be fair, and I must satisfy my conscience with that consideration.

But to come to Father McSwiney, who wrote a letter of two columns in length, which I gave in its entirety. He had much to say upon many things, including English misrule, Irish agitations, and the Fenians, but the burthen of his song, as the burthen of the song of his *confrères* then and since, was Tenant Right. That was the panacea to be got, as he thought, by Dr. Cullen's new agitation. But it was not got by that, but by far other things. However, we have this Tenant Right now, including, I fear, some landlord wrong, and our woes seem to us numerous as ever. Here is my short comment upon his long letter :—

"We may reply to our reverend correspondent's letter, after Cicero's and his own fashion, by asking *cui bono?* We have answered him by anticipation about the new agitation, and he must excuse us for not answering him at all about the 'Fenians.' He knows the Government knows all about them, and that ought to satisfy him. In fact he knows everything, and we couldn't be so cruel as to deprive our readers of so much wisdom." This was, perhaps, smart, but it was certainly flippant, and I cannot now look upon it as fair, when I come to read what he said about the Fenians, part of which was this:—"I have no hatred for Fenians. On the contrary, I believe that the great majority, *at least of the young men* who join that party, are the best and bravest of the Irish race. They see how fallen is their country, and they would strive to raise her. Love of country is not a crime. Patriotism was implanted in man's heart by God." There was, perhaps, some sting in the words I have italicized, but the spirit of the whole was so good that I should have overlooked them and much else in the letter. Father McSwiney, unlike most of his fellows, was neither vituperative nor vindictive, and was strictly within his rights in thinking the Fenians foolish, as I was within mine in thinking him not over wise, if only I had said so in a less flippant and more fitting manner. I make here, however, this late *amende*, knowing not whether or not he is here to read it, but fearing that he, like so many of our friends and enemies of that olden time, may long since have gone to another and a better world. But even so his ghost may be gratified by that open confession which is proverbially, and I think truly, supposed to be good for the soul.

Here I must skip over several numbers of the paper, extracting nothing, though absorbing much. We have, of course, the usual accounts of denunciations, tampering with our agents, refusal of sacraments, and the like, and much comment upon all this by Kickham and others, but mostly involving mere temporary matters, or assuming much knowledge of men and things of the day. Much also there was in our leading columns, largely by myself, on agitations and agitators, the English Parliament, and the people we sent there. And this is a sort of retrospective reading of a most melancholy if more or less instructive kind; patent and blatant humbug on the part of our own M.P.'s, and insolent patronage or ignorant abuse on the part of English members. Nor were our agitators out of Parliament any more in earnest, while they were often even more ridiculous. But the difficulty now is to make most of these people well enough known to be worth laughing at. We have too many fools and rogues of our own time to laugh at or cry over. Let the old fools and rogues, then, in so far as they were merely what they were, rest in peace. We shall only disentomb them when they can be made to teach some definite lesson to the present time.

In the eighteenth number of our second volume

Kickham writes fully on a "card"[1] of Archbishop[2] Purcell, of Cincinnati, which had just appeared in his paper, the *Catholic Telegraph.* "Archbishop Purcell says he originally condemned the Fenian Brotherhood because it was oath-bound. And now having discovered that it is not oath-bound, he condemns it all the same. He says the pledge of membership is equivalent to the strongest kind of oath. We have repeatedly said that all this talk about oaths was simply a pretence. It would be a crime to go to work in earnest for Ireland with or without an oath. The Irish bishops condemned all brotherhoods whether bound by oath or not; and here is an American bishop declaring the words 'I solemnly pledge my sacred word of honour as a truthful and honest man,' equivalent to the strongest kind of oath." Kickham goes on to tell us that the Archbishop had two other objections to the Fenian Brotherhood; first, that it was not democratic enough, and secondly, that if Ireland were freed by the Fenians, "they would give her a worse constitution and make her condition worse than it is at present." The Archbishop, in the

[1] This appears to be American for a shorter sort of pastoral or other manifesto.

[2] This is the prelate, who, some twenty years later, in conjunction with his brother, the Archdeacon, made away with some millions of dollars entrusted to his care. The American Press, I remember, treated the Archbishop with much greater leniency than, I think, he deserved. He did not, no doubt, apply the money to his own use, but there was the most criminal neglect on his part, and criminal meddling and muddling on the part of the Archdeacon, his brother, to whom the Bishop had entrusted the management of the money, much of which appears to have gone in the building of churches and the like.

self-same "card," says he wishes to see Ireland "free from the galling yoke of England's injustice, inhumanity, and tyranny." The democratic objection Kickham simply treats with contempt. A people struggling to be free cannot organize itself after the same fashion as a people in the possession of freedom. Of the Archbishop's fears and wishes he says: "We find it hard to believe him. We can more easily understand some of his brother prelates who consider the defects of the British constitution to be like the spots on the sun.[1] To turn to other things, of less importance indeed, but still of some, I find myself writing an article, on the 1st of April, headed "More English Amenities." From this I may quote a portion of the last paragraph; not the best part of the article, but the most intelligible apart from the context: "But, after all, it matters little what Englishmen think or say about us, save in so far as it influences the thought or actions of Irishmen. . . . The Irishmen who abuse England most are not those who love Ireland best. Abuse of England is too often but the mere stock-in-trade of canting agitators[2]—frequently the imperfect utterance of the illiterate. But abuse of Ireland flows glibly from the mouths of noble lords, and honourable

[1] This is, if my memory does not fail me, an allusion to some utterance of Bishop Moriarty, the amiable prelate who thought hell was not hot enough, nor eternity long enough, for the punishment of the Fenians.

[2] Queerly enough, the canting agitator has changed his stock-in-trade since. Now he sings the praise of the Saxon. He is all for the Union of Hearts and full of faith in the English democracy. But 'tis only the Englishman who believes him, and in him is only listening to the echo of his (the Englishman's) own unwisdom.

M.P.'s and able editors. What will the fastidious people spoken of above (people whom I spoke of as constantly crying out, not without some show of reason, against Irish abuse of the Saxon) say to this parting shot from the Pall Mall battery? 'Your true aboriginal Celt has got so used to potting something large from behind a hedge, that if landlords were driven out, and neither wolves nor bears introduced as substitutes, we fear he would be taking liberties with his next door neighbour.'" There is another article in the same number, by I know not whom, which dwells on a matter which calls for even louder remonstrance at the present time. "Why so much should be said about tenant right, and so little about anybody else's right, is what agitators alone may understand, but what we are sure no one else can. 'Tisn't that the tenant farmer is in a more wretched condition than the farm labourer or the mechanic. There are comparatively few tenant farmers, we are sure, who are obliged to live on a meal a day of the worse kind of food, yet there are thousands of labourers and mechanics who couldn't probably recollect when they ate one full meal in the twenty-four hours," and so on, with much more about food, firing, and clothing. Again, and here I think I can detect the idyllic touch of Kickham: "Are the labouring poor of this country content to be thus for ever outcasts and paupers? Shall they never possess as much of their native soil as would sod a lark, while strangers occupy thousands of acres? *Cruel landlords* and *ambitious tenants* have blotted out every trace of our once numerous cottiers. Sheep and bullocks now roam over once happy hearths, and browse beneath old outspreading hawthorn of the happy long ago; while those who once sat around that hearth or beneath that outspreading hawthorn, are now crouching in some desolate garret or demoralizing pauper palace."

The italics above are mine, and I do not see why the landlords should be cruel while the tenants were only ambitious. However, the fact is there, a fact I do not remember to have seen noticed in public during the great agrarian struggle of the last dozen years, while I do well remember the impression produced on my own mind, some years ago, by a drive round the town of Charleville, in the company and under the guidance of the late Canon Rice, where I saw the traces of the numberless cottages, levelled not by the *cruel* landlords but by the ambitious tenants, and could afterwards verify the contrast drawn by Kickham between the once happy hearths and the wretched slums into which these victims of ambition were driven.[1]

I do not know but my reader may be growing weary of all these extracts from the *Irish People*. I am not giving them as gems of style or as mines of thought, but mainly to supply a generation that knows us not with

[1] I am no *advocatus diaboli* here. The landlord is no doubt often heartless, but I think still oftener careless and reckless; still I cannot in the least gather that he is as a rule any worse than the farmer, especially the big one; and yet down to the very time at which I write your "able editor" and unable agitator will have it that nearly every landlord is next door to a devil, while most tenants are as near an approach as possible to angels. That was not Kickham's notion, strong tenant-righter as he was, nor is it mine.

some materials for forming an opinion about us. The paper is quite un-come-at-able by the reader of the present day. Of course, there are stray volumes or numbers to be found here and there about the country, and some no doubt in public libraries,[1] but these can but satisfy the curiosity of few. I think, then, a little prolixity is pardonable, and possibly may be even meritorious. I am not, of course, a quite unprejudiced judge on this matter, and if I should find a friend or friends candid enough to tell me that I have overdone the thing, I have it always in my power to strike out, "boil down," or otherwise abridge my narrative.

Of course, I have other and more practical objects. I think, and many think with me, that the light still needs to be spread, and that much of our doctrine needs enforcement as greatly now as when we wrote. Hence the peculiar prominence given to Kickham, and the comparative putting into the background of Luby and myself. But the reader must not be allowed to forget that we also had our say, as continuously and mostly as lengthily as Kickham, whether as forcibly or pertinently or not, said reader must judge for himself. As I have said before, we allowed Kickham, as a good Catholic, to tackle the priests. Not that we questioned our own right. The matter was one partly of convenience or expedience. You have quite as much right to judge a priest in politics if you disbelieve in the doctrines of the Council of Trent as if you believe in them. Still, con-

[1] I know that the British Museum has but an imperfect copy; only the first volume, I understand.

demnation generally comes more forcibly from one's co-religionists.

Here is a paragraph from the twenty-fourth number of our second volume, which has a strong bearing upon the present and upon all time, as well as upon that stormy past in which Luby wrote it. His theme was "Noble Irishwomen." "But the influence of woman appears in its grandest form, when a true and noble-hearted wife endeavours to sustain and cheer, in the dark hour of trial and discouragement, the hopes and faith of her husband. In every struggle for country, or for any other grand object, moments arise when the whole horizon is black, clouds wrap the future, and difficulties appear insuperable. This is the time when doubts spring to life in the bravest and most resolute hearts. For a moment, perhaps, the heroic soul is tempted to yield to despair. Should the patriot's wife be unworthy of him then—should she be selfish, or even narrowly attached to her mere family—his human weakness will have a hair's-breadth escape, if it do not yield to temptation. In such an hour, more precious than gold seven times purified in the furnace is the heroic wife who points to the path of honour and fidelity, and encourages her husband to trample under foot difficulties, doubts, despair itself. Happy, in the higher and truer sense, and glorious the woman, who would rather see her husband in chains or dead than see him abandon the cause of truth and justice, and his comrades in that cause, in the hour of trial and danger. Happy and thrice blest the man who marches through life cheered on by such a wife; and happy, too, the children born of their love." And thrice blest was Luby in having such a wife who, when she saw her husband "in chains" if not dead, failed not nor faltered for one moment, but bore his fate and her own as only a heroine could, keeping still the even tenor of her way, ever helpful to him and to all who with him had suffered in the cause, while ever mindful of the sacred duty to "the children born of their love."[1] Luby goes on to ask, "Are there many women of this noble type in Ireland to-day?" We hope, nay, we fondly trust, there are. Well he and I know there were some, and I believe with him there were many, as I hope and trust there are many in the Ireland of to-day; but the women of these days are not tried as were the women of those.

To pass from Luby to myself, which is seldom going very far in spirit, separated as we have mostly been in the flesh, but in this case the transition is "from grave to gay" and in a sense "from lively to severe." Instead of dealing with "Noble Irishwomen," I took for my theme, in a short article called "Gigmen on Men," a rather ignoble class of Irishmen. As we have gigmen as well as men always among us, there may, perhaps, be no harm in giving even now some part of what I said then. "We have heard a good deal from time to time of the contempt felt or feigned by aristocratic shop-

[1] I cannot help here coupling with the name of Mrs. Luby that of her friend and my sister. Her task was not perhaps so hard as Mrs. Luby's, but that task, as all tasks, she fulfilled as few women could. To God and Ireland she was ever sternly true, and to me, through life and unto death, she was all that human heart or head could desire.

keepers, attorneys, parish priests, and others of the *haute monde*, for the social status of the mythological Fenian. It is currently rumoured that the number of rebels who keep gigs is scandalously small, and the above-mentioned aristocrats are wild at the thought that men of such little means should engage in so large an adventure. A great many of the gig-keeping critics don't disapprove of the thing to be done if only it could be done decorously; but what can a sensible shopkeeper think of an enterprise which is presumably unsupported by the well-to-do classes? Let a few [1] "men of station," aldermen or others, raise the green flag once more, and the respectabilities will, of course, flock round their standards. We ourselves, with the greatest anxiety to get at the bottom of this subject of station, to know why one man is fit to act with or under and another not, find our mind more and more confused on the matter. What is it that constitutes station in the Ireland of to-day? We could at least understand if we did not sympathize with the old heraldic notions,[2] but it seems we have changed all that now. It appears to be somewhat disreputable to keep a small shop in a village, but quite meritorious

[1] Here one is reminded of the notable saying of Wolfe Tone, "If the men of property won't join us, then we must fall back upon that highly respectable class of the community, the men of no property." "Men of station" was a phrase used by the late John Dillon, and "aldermen or others" is a sneer at the aldermanic, if scarcely aristocratic, Dillon.

[2] I believe I not only understood but did sympathize with these old notions. There is much in what we call the "good dhrop," as in the saying of our French cousins that *le bon sang ne peut mentir*." What I did not understand then, and do not now, is why one man should be thought better than another simply because he is better off.

to keep a large one in town. A curate cannot conceal his contempt for a man who does tailoring on a small scale in a village; and an archbishop shows respect, bordering on reverence, for a man who does tailoring on a large scale in a city. Hence it appears that it is not what we are, or even what our grandmothers were, but the money we make, that makes all the difference.

> 'rem facias, rem
> Si possis, recte; si non, quocunque modo rem.'

The man in the village may be clever, kindly, and courteous, yet he is *caviare* to the curate, while a bank book opens all doors—at least clears all platforms—to the man in the city."

We have changed all this somewhat of late, though I do not know that it is at all for the better. Our later day agitators have been obliged to fall back on the men of "no property" with a vengeance. Hence our wonderful '86, to mention no others. No one could accuse them of means any more than merit or worth. But there was a great difference between the relation of Wolfe Tone and ourselves to the "men of no property" and the relation of the agitators to the same class, or the same class to the agitators. We called upon men to risk life and liberty, with little or no chance of gain in this world, and there was no reason in the nature of things why men with small purses should not have big hearts and stout arms. But when, if not by leaders, at least by the force of circumstances, the appeal is made only to the lower passions, and one is called upon not to risk his own life or liberty, but rather to endanger the properties and lives of other people, then you will certainly have many "men of no property," and many of little, on your side, but one could scarcely even laughingly call them "that respectable portion of the community." But comparisons are proverbially odious, however occasionally useful.

And perhaps the reader will think it is full time for me to get back to Fenianism in its more practical form. But that I cannot do quite yet. I must do this book in my own way or not at all, and though possibly it were better it were not done at all, if it is to be done, then it must be done discursively, irregularly, and intermittently. Whether there be art in all this, or the art to conceal art, I cannot well know; but that there is nature—my nature at least—that I do know, and I have no inclination to strive to drive it away with a fork or any other implement.

Happily, too, for such readers as may feel they have had enough of the paper, I have got through it till within some three months of its violent extinction. Most, then, of what I take it to have been and done I have necessarily told already, and what further remains to be said by way of extract or comment I at least mean to make brief.

In the twenty-eighth number of our second volume, amid much about America and the close of the civil war, we find Kickham dealing with the priests, not from his usual point of view, but from one which has unfortunately a permanent, if not the most permanent, interest for all of us. "The *only* argument[1] we ever heard in favour of the interference of priests in elections is, that they counteract the authority of the landlords. But it is a well-known fact that priests have been far more violent in their opposition to popular candidates than the rankest Orangemen. Let us instance their furious denunciations of Mr. G. H. Moore, in Kilkenny, some years ago, when Father Tom O'Shea exclaimed, 'It is not the people but the priests who are rotten.' We'd be sorry to see Mr. Moore turning up again as a parliamentary candidate; but if he took such a notion into his head, he'd find bishops and priests arrayed against him. It is gratifying to think that not *one really good Irishman* wishes to become a member of the English Parliament." The italics are mine, not Kickham's. Of course he uses "good Irishman" in the rather technical sense of good nationalist, and in that sense what he said was true. Good men in every sense, like the late John Martin, for instance, have gone there since, and in a fashion good use has been made of even the bad men, and things have been materially altered by the ballot and the extended suffrage, so that now you can make some sort of an implement of war out of your M.P., and that, too, without calling upon the people to make any sacrifices in its production. Still, the implement is but a brittle one at best, very liable to break and wound the

[1] This argument has of course, since the Ballot Act, ceased to be an argument at all, and the continued interference of priests in elections is a scandal pure and simple, which is melancholy to me, not so much for what it shows the priests to be, as for what it shows the people to be.

hand that wields it, leaving untouched and uninjured the force against which it should be impelled. Again, leaving doubtful metaphors aside, your M.P. as M.P. is next to nothing, though as individual thinker or actor, as a Burke or a Parnell, he may be much. But it is no present business of mine to show what M.P.'s are, or what can be made of them, but merely to point out that, however it may be now, they were, when Kickham wrote, simply "a mockery, a delusion, and a snare."

CHAPTER XXI.

CONTEMPORARY TALK ABOUT THE FENIANS.

But to turn from M.P.'s and priests to my more proper theme of Fenians. When I shall have brought what I may call my review of the paper to an end, I shall have more to say of them, but, *en attendant,* I may say a word or two about them as they directly crop up in the paper; indirectly, of course, in their unconstitutional and anti-clerical attitude, they were always there, and especially in the correspondence columns.

In the thirteenth number of our second volume, I find two articles, respectively called "Fenianism Metamorphosed" and "Facts about the Fenians"; the first, I fancy, written by Kickham, and the second by myself. The first article is chiefly occupied with a description of the changed tone of the papers with regard to Fenianism. But a short time before, the Fenians were held to be a drunken, disorderly, and generally disreputable set. But now all that was changed with our writing people, who, as Kickham phrased it, had now come to hold that "Fenianism shuns the public-house and gives the police barrack a wide berth, and so far from the 'Fenian' being remarkable for an unsteadiness of gait, he may now be known by his measured tread and upright, soldierly bearing. 'Fenianism is no longer laughed at. It is an ugly fact.' So say the newspapers."

So far Kickham was but translating and summarizing the newspapers. Farther on in his article he goes on to say, on what authority it is not now easy for me to know, but, from all I could ever gather, with perfect truth, that "drunkenness and faction-fighting are disappearing. Our young men are becoming more intelligent and manly, and, consequently, more moral every day; and this change is most apparent precisely in those places where the *Irish People* is most read and 'Fenianism' is said most to abound. The most ignorant can scarcely be persuaded that the thing which produces such fruit can be as black as it is painted."

But, if I am to judge by my own article, the seriousness of Fenianism was chiefly felt at home. The Britishers, as usual, were late in learning anything about us. I was commenting on an article from the *Times*, which I had copied into the paper, and anent which I said: "The *Times* is not usually very successful in its comic efforts, but when Ireland is its theme, anything may pass for fun with its English readers. That, however, is more their affair than ours. Thin-skinned people here will sometimes be irritated by the small sneers of the English press, but we thank our stars we are not thin-skinned, and any amount of bad jokes can make little difference in our estimation of the amiable country that condescends to govern us (for our good) against our will."

The first of the *Times* facts was that "the Fenians are

an American society, formed in the United States." That fact I willingly admitted, but it seems it was about the only fact I found in the *Times* article. The second *fact* is, that while the Fenians say they are not a secret body, they claim to be so very secretly organized "that the sharpest spy in the world could never betray them." Upon which my comment is, that "considering that a *Times* reporter can get at all about them, it clearly does not require much sharpness to betray them." But, of course, the answer was that the Fenians made no such claims at all. A number of "facts," too, were given about the Americans in their supposed relationship to Fenians, such as that the latter "have fallen upon evil days just now. Treason happens to be terribly out of fashion in the land of their adoption." Again, "the Americans have had Wolfe Tones and Emmets of their own, and they have shot them down in battle or locked them up in dungeons." To which I replied that "they haven't, however, hanged their Emmets yet, but the *Times* plainly thinks they'll not only hang their own Emmets, but help to hang other people's, and the opinion of the *Times* on American matters carries great weight. Our soul is sick with terror at the thought of what President Johnson may do with John O'Mahony." Some more of what I then gave my readers of the *Times* I may perhaps as well give here again. The *Times* we have always with us, and it hasn't grown wiser as the years have gone by, nor is it less typical of the average Englishman of the more or less thinking class now than it was then. Here, anyway, is how it thought then.

"What is it that an 'Irish' Government or a 'National' Government, or an Independent Government would do for Ireland that the present Government will not do? If Irishmen run away from their native land, so do Englishmen, and with precisely the same purpose, viz. that of bettering themselves. An Irishman can go where he pleases and say what he likes" (this is rather funny reading to me now, when I think of where I was sent shortly after, mainly, if not entirely, for saying some of the things I liked, but which the English authorities did not like). "Englishmen are ready to help Irishmen in making Ireland more productive if Irishmen will allow them. It would be wiser to turn these conditions to account than to ascend to a fabulous age for an imaginary advantage. *What we have to do with is Ireland, not Phœnicia.* The Irish people are as acute as any people in the world, and we do not believe that any man among them can put faith in the idea of Ireland for the Fenians! 'Ireland for the Elks' would be about as sensible a cry."

To which all I had to say at the time was, that the words that I have italicized above were the second *fact* in the articles, and I don't know that I need add anything else by way of comment now, save to notice, for English readers, the slight confusion in the *Times* man's mind between a race of Irish heroes and a country with which their only connection was a slightly phonetic one. As to the cry of Ireland for the Fenians—a cry never heard save by the *Times*—and the fact acknowledged by the *Times* that no man in Ireland put faith in it, presumably not even a Fenian, the confusion of mind here is, as such men as the *Times* scribe would say, quite Hibernian. But all that stuff is only a specimen of the sort of thing to which we are habitually treated by our British brethren. Not that I ever complained of it. Quite the contrary. I gave as much of it as I could find to my readers, and mostly without comment.

In passing over the pages of our paper, I come, a couple of numbers farther on (1st July, 1865), upon something which is not without interest in this connection. It is from the New York *Daily News*, and was written by John Mitchel. The article is headed "Fenians," and is largely occupied with Darcy McGee and what Mitchel took to be his mission, about which, by the way, I have up to this said little here, though I said much in the paper at the time. After describing, quite accurately, I think, the sort of man and Irishman McGee was, Mitchel goes on to say that 'In the present alarm about Fenianism, this being is naturally employed to go to Ireland and preach it down. The London *Times* is delighted. This is the sort of Irishman that the *Times* loves—a rational, sensible, practical Irishman, who exhorts his countrymen to submit to Anglo-Saxon dominion, and hold their foolish tongues for 'a pack of fools.'[1]

"As for the Irish in the United States, he assures his

[1] This is the phrase used by McGee of himself and the other men of 1848, in which, as both Mitchel and I said at the time, he did himself at least the very greatest injustice, for there is not a scintilla of doubt (in my mind at least) but that he (McGee) belonged to quite a different category of mankind.

countrymen (to the *Times'* great delight) that those are 'spoiled Irish,' and as for the Fenians, they are 'Bedlamites.'

"It is amazing," Mitchel goes on to add, "what a very large number there are of these same Bedlamites and spoiled Irishmen. The *Times* says that in Ireland the Brotherhood is invisible, and must have used firm seed; not adverting to the fact that it is not intended to be visible to British eyes at present. In fact, the *Times* obviously knows nothing whatever about the matter; not so much as the meaning of the name, which it declares means *Phœnician.* That journal seems to have learned nothing on the subject, except from a highly sensational and poetic account of the matter lately given by a New York journal, which deals in 'Startling Developments,' but which knew about as little of the affair as the *Times* itself. Now, we could give the London *Times* much information on this subject; could tell the real meaning of the name 'Fenian'; and give a rational account (not in poetry, but in prose) of the true objects of the Brotherhood. But, in fact, it does not court newspaper popularity at present; it is not a 'startling development' or an 'immense sensation,' just yet. At the first note of war between England and the United States, upon any argument, no doubt it will be both the one and the other."

No doubt it would have been; but that war was not to be. A few words I may as well perhaps say here about Mitchel, though he scarcely enters directly into my story, or the story of Fenianism, until after I had ceased to have any part in it, save what I could take in thought from behind the prison bars of Pentonville and Portland.

Some time, however, after the publication[1] of the article from which I have quoted above, Mitchel was arrested by the United States Government, on considerations I need not enter into here. He was, I believe, the only Southern partisan the Government thought fit to imprison, with the single exception of the President of the Southern Confederacy. He could not, however, have spent many months in prison, for I remember to have read, probably near the end of November, shortly before my trial, that Mitchel had left New York for Paris, as the accredited agent and emissary of the Fenian Brotherhood. What he did there I knew little of till afterwards, when I heard much of it from my sister and others. To make a long story short, Mitchel, after a while in Paris, began to grow more or less dissatisfied, if by no means with the principles, most certainly with the prospects, and very much with the *personnel*, of Fenianism. Stephens he never could endure, and the dislike was mutual, and this to my mind was much of a fault in both of them; not that they should not like each other, which was probably a matter beyond their control, but that, spite of likings and dislikings, they could not act together, strongly if not heartily, against the foe they both hated. Anyway, though I am more or less antici-

[1] On the 14th of June, as I find in a subsequent issue of our paper. Of course, publication in New York and not in Dublin is meant.

pating, they, conjointly or severally, did little for the cause in France. Neither of them was a Tone, nor were the times propitious. As to why Stephens failed to effect anything in France, 'tis not for me to tell here; but as to Mitchel, I may say that he was ever a power, or rather, perhaps, a strong influence, in Irish affairs, not as an actor, but as a writer and a thinker; and as, happily for us, the written word remains, and his word will long remain, he will still move and stir the Irish soul long after all the brawling windbags and leaden scribblers of the day have gone the way alike of the great and the small.

CHAPTER XXII.

A GENERAL ELECTION.

DURING all these summer months of 1865 the country was in the throes of preparation for a general election; all that was blatant and insincere expanding itself in addresses over the advertising columns of the newspapers, and the foolish and self-seeking all the country over open-mouthed (in every sense of the word) and otherwise active in the strife. We, as the reader may imagine, took no interest, or only a malign one, in all this. Parliamentary representation had reached that state in Ireland that no honest man, not a fool or a prophet, could well see anything but the most disastrous outlook from it. Anyway, to us at least the difference was strictly 'twixt Tweedledum and Tweedledee. All were not, of course, quite insignificant, but nearly all were, and if you sought for honesty even in a limited sense, you must look for it in the ranks of the so-called enemies of the country (Conservatives and the like, for there was no clear issue then, save our very clear and altogether unparliamentary one, between the Union and its Repeal, in part or in whole), and not in those of its so-called friends.

But the trouble, and worry, and worse was there, and some notice we took of it incidentally now and then. Here is, for instance, what I said briefly enough, I think, on the Queen's Speech, in our paper of July 8th. "Her Majesty, the Queen of England, has just said her say—by deputy, of course—to her Parliament before dismissing it. Her Majesty seems to be immensely satisfied with the world in general, and her North American subjects in particular. Perhaps it is enough for us to say that it is very easy to satisfy Her Majesty." But if I was brief, I find the Queen was, as usual, lengthy enough, taking up two-thirds of a column, in small type, of our paper, and roamed nearly all the world over without letting her eye for one moment rest on Ireland. The United States, Canada, India, and Prussia find mention in the speech, but no word can I see bearing even incidentally on Ireland. Not that I complain now of all that any more than I did at the time. The least said by the Queen as well as by all other British people about Ireland the soonest mended. I notice the fact chiefly to show how little of the prophetic Her Majesty's inspirers had. They saw no need to give even a word to Ireland, yet how many days and months, and even years, have they given since, and when will they have done with her? Nor should it be forgotten just now that the eloquent, if rather verbose, old man whom we have still amongst us was then, perhaps, the second man in importance in Her Majesty's Government.

Coming to what we said about elections or candidates, 'tisn't easy to be at once short and clear at this distance of time. I must confine myself to some little said about some few men still known to us. In the paper, for instance, preceding the one from which I have last quoted, I find an article called "Claptrap Candidates," where I deal somewhat, *apropos* of an almost grotesque article in the *Pall Mall Gazette,* with Mr. (afterwards Sir) John Pope Hennessy. The *Pall Mall,* after likening Mr. Hennessy to the Irishman of the story who was always "agin" the Government, and basing the comparison upon the fact that Mr Hennessy said, in his address, that he would never support any Government which did not unite, instead of dividing, Irish interests, the *Pall Mall* man goes on to indite the following almost incredible nonsense. "*Consequently,* Mr. Pope Hennessy will, like his compatriot, be opposed to the Government *qua* Government; will vote against it, not because it has done anything or left anything undone, but simply because it exists. There speaks the true Irishman, the man who can recognize anything except a fact, believe anything except a truism, and strive for anything except a definite object. Suppose we had a Parliament of Pope Hennessys! It would be very like the Parliament which would assemble in Dublin after Repeal." It is needless, if it would not be useless, to give my comment on this. 'Tis only a good specimen of the sort of thing your funny Englishman constantly gives us about Irishmen; and your writing Englishman, on this theme, is always striving after the amusing, save, on the not unfrequent occasions, when he is fiercely indignant.

But to turn from the *Pall Mall* man to Pope

Hennessy—the Hennessy of fact, not of fiction. I do not know that there is any harm in showing how one young Irishman looked to another some thirty "golden years ago." "Mr. Hennessy is, we understand, what used to be called a Young Englander—a queer kind of thing for an Irishman to be. He is, at any rate, a great admirer of Mr. Disraeli, and an active Tory partisan; quite free, we believe, from that antipathy to future administrations attributed to him by the *Pall Mall Gazette.* He is, also, a young gentleman with a most excellent opinion of his own intellect and acquirements. He was no sooner called to the Bar than he began to lecture Sir Roundell Palmer and Sir Hugh Cairns on the laws of England, and he now proposes to preserve the Irish race by putting in the Tories. 'Ireland,' says Mr. Hennessy, 'will be the question for the new Parliament.' To which we may answer, possibly, but most certainly the new Parliament is not the question for Ireland. He goes on to say that 'our people are rapidly leaving the country,' that 'the Queen's ministers refused to express the slightest regret for the grievous decline of the population,' and that, therefore, 'they are unworthy of our confidence.' This is all very well, indeed, but the people of the King's County are greater fools than we take them for, if they are ready to swallow Mr. Hennessy's implied, though not expressed, conclusion, that the Tories are sorry for the emigration and most anxious to stop it." So I wrote, I think not unfairly, at the time of Pope Hennessy. I have, however, come to think much better of him since, while, of course, having no sympathy with his career, in so far as it was spent in the service of England. Some couple of years after this, when I was in the grip of the enemy, he spoke out manfully (being, I believe, the first public man so to speak) in defence of the Fenian prisoners, and many years after he wrote a very interesting book,[1] full of good Irish spirit and feeling. Besides, as an administrator, he always leant towards the oppressed, who were mostly the mass of the people in all the colonies where he governed and the English ruled, and by so doing mostly brought down upon himself the wrath of the average Englishman, who (like the average man everywhere) is necessarily a fool, and (like himself) but too often more or less of a brute. While still then objecting as strongly as ever to an Irishman's attaining wealth (or at least competence) and title in the service of England, I can now do John Pope Hennessy the justice of believing that he would have far preferred gaining either, even if in a lesser degree, in the service of his own country. I am verging perhaps upon verbosity here; first, from a desire to be just to an eminent Irishman who has just gone from amongst us, and secondly, because in writing of Hennessy I am, in a sense, though very indirectly, autobiographic. He was a part, though a very small one, of my early life. He had been at the Cork College at the same time as I was, and though I did not know him then, at the time of which I write I had some acquaintance with him, and knew still more of him from having many common friends and

[1] "Raleigh in Ireland."

acquaintances.[1] By some accident we never met afterwards, though he sought me out in France; but I have certainly ever had a kindly feeling for him since I left prison.

I pass on to a far more eminent man and probably a better Irishman than Pope Hennessy, of whom I was obliged to speak somewhat at this time, *apropos* of elections, candidates, canvassing, and the like. I am alluding to Mr. Butt, then and long before a well-known figure in Irish politics, but since far better known and far more highly esteemed by most Irishmen abroad and at home. I do not know that I said much against Mr. Butt at this time, though something, as the reader will see, I did say, and a great deal I might easily have said, had sufficient cause for so doing arisen; for, up to that time, his character, both as a public and a private man, had been of the shakiest.

What, however, I find myself first saying about Mr. Butt's candidature for Youghal has much more to do with elections in general and priests in particular. Here is some of it. "Mr. Butt is, we believe, a bit of a humbug, but he has certainly been badly treated in Youghal. He was ready to go in for the three points of the charter,[2] and to pledge himself to remain in opposi-

[1] I particularly remember that he was the first person who got me, some time about 1860, I fancy, into the House of Commons, as also how little edified I was by that institution.

[2] This is what I used to call the three chief planks in the platform of Dr. Cullen's new association—which were Catholic education, Disestablishment of the Church, and some measure of Tenant Right.

tion till they were ceded. He has, however, the fatal fault of being poor. He cannot build bridges, and has possibly but sparingly (perhaps 'slightly' would be the better word, for close-fistedness is scarcely one of Mr. Butt's faults) subscribed to the local religious institutions. Mr. Butt's opponent is the persistent Mr. McKenna, who has hit upon the right place at last. He has bought property near Youghal, he has given a free bridge, and, best of all, he has won over the priests." A little after, in the same article, I leave Mr. Butt and Mr. McKenna, and proceed to talk of the ever-present and mostly ever-pressing question of "priests in politics." "But it matters nothing to us that a rich banker should sit for Youghal instead of a poor barrister. What matters much is the conduct of priests in politics. The parish priest of Tralee, a well-known anti-Nationalist, supports the professing rebel, the O'Donoghue, rather than the professing loyalist, Mr. McKenna, while the parish priest of Youghal, the fiery League letter-writer and denouncer of England, can easily swallow the self-same Mr. McKenna, loyalty and all. It is needless to carry on the comparison to curates. While, however, we are on the subject of priests in politics, it may be no harm to notice a strange production, from the pen of the Rev. Thaddeus O'Malley,[1] which appeared in the last *Irishman*. This

[1] A strange man, well-nigh forgotten, I should say, by the present generation. He was, if not the father of Federalism, its ever-consistent and persistent supporter. I am far from praising him for this, or, indeed, particularly for anything; his head seems to me to have been mostly wrong, his heart not over right, and his conscience, if I am to judge by the passage given above, casuistical in the worst sense of the word.

gentleman, with singular insight into the character of the candidates and constituency of Cashel, suggests to the former the propriety of retiring in favour of Mr. Gavan Duffy, and plainly preaches to the latter the morality practised by Father Maher. No elector should imagine that his hands are tied by any promise of his vote to any individual; 'for no such promise should ever be given but with the reservation—if no better man should offer.' With such and such like sayings and doings crowding in upon us from all quarters, we must be still excused for holding, Father John Power of Powerstown notwithstanding, that the interests of Catholicity as well as country would be best served by the non-interference of priests in politics."

This was one of the very few occasions on which I personally dealt with the theme of priests in politics, and I said nothing then that I should not say now, and nothing, alas! that does not need to be said now. Of course, I read and approved of all that Kickham wrote, but I had in no sense inspired it. His thoughts were his own, as was his manner of expressing them. Unquestioning Catholic though he was, he had no more notion of taking his politics from the priest than from the parson, and saw no reason why people should, but rather indeed much reason—gathered from the history of his country and especially of its immediate past—why they should not.

Reverting to Mr. Butt. I should not now say that he was a "bit of a humbug." He had many serious faults, both as a man and a leader of men, but I believe he loved Ireland in his own way, and he certainly did much during his later years to advance, or at least support, the National cause. But then he moved fast and far after the time I wrote, and indeed the birth of his Nationalism (in any real sense of the word) might be said to date from the Fenian trials, which began not many months after, and which, I understand, had something to do with his conversion. Of course I saw much of Butt on my own trial, but never after, though it was by mere accident that I missed meeting him several years ago in Dublin.

But enough, or nearly enough, about elections. They concerned us little if at all, and, consequently, we concerned ourselves but slightly with them, and I have treated of the matter mainly in relation to a few men who played some part in the world's affairs since.

In our paper of July 29th I find that the farce had been played out by that time, and I read some general remarks, due, I should say, to Kickham, upon the net result of the performance. "The late elections," he says, "have proved that the people of Ireland have lost all faith in Parliamentary agitation." Well, they seemed to prove that, but then the Irish people, like all other peoples, have very shifting faiths, that is, ever changing and varying as regards methods and men, but never, I believe, altering as to the end in view. We always struggle, with however varying energy and earnestness, to free ourselves from England, and we move in the direction we wish, or not at all, just as we find the right men or the right methods, and rather more in the first case than in the last; for with the right man all methods are in a measure effective, whereas with the wrong man, however right may be the theory, in practice things are sure to come to next to nothing in the long run. To come from the abstract to the concrete. When we get a Tone or a Stephens, an O'Connell or a Parnell, we live and act, and the result is never quite *nil*. I institute no comparisons, either between the men themselves, or between them and the rut of leaders. They were men at least, and not mannikins.

CHAPTER XXIII.

A VERY RAMBLING CHAPTER.

STEPHENS we had then, and I am trying, in this book, vainly perhaps, to show what came of him, and Parnell we have had since, but between a real unconstitutional method and a real constitutional one we were destined, as ever, to have a sham one, or rather a series of sham ones, and here is something of what Kickham thought of one of them: "We said from the first that the 'National Association' was intended to support the Whigs. No one can doubt now that we were right. The policy of 'Independent Opposition' was a fraud. The pass was sold and the Whigs let in everywhere, while the real 'Independent Opposition' candidates were left in the lurch, as in Kilkenny and Wexford. The man who should vote for Mr. Pope Hennessy was threatened with 'a visible curse,' because Mr. Pope Hennessy was not a Whig. But the Association refused to recommend the electors of Dungarvan to abstain from voting for the Law Adviser of the Castle, because the Law Adviser of the Crown was a Whig. In like manner, the Solicitor-General of the Whigs was supported at Mallow."

And so on, and so on. In another article, written by I know not whom, but certainly not by myself, we are told that "two great evils have again been exhibited to the eyes of a disgusted world by the late sublime farces, which, under the name of elections, have been enacted in this country." One was of course that landlord influence which the ballot has put an end to; the second, as the article says, is "the prostitution of that sacred power over the conscience of the people with which ecclesiastics are clothed, in order to procure the return of those favoured candidates who will get places and pensions for 'nephews' and 'cousins,' and promote pet projects about denominational education while Ireland is perishing." Here what I may call the loaves and fishes' side of the "priests in politics" question is put plainly, and I have little doubt will have to be put again as long as priests remain in politics. It is one thing to use, or rather abuse, your sacred power for mere political ends, but it is a far baser thing to use that sacred power for mere self-interest.

I take up my narrative again, after another of these long intervals of inactivity which are for ever intermittently recurring during the course of this book. I feel indeed as if I were nearing the goal, but, alas! I cannot know when I shall reach it, or through what turnings, shiftings, and windings I may still have to pass. I am not a machine, but a man, and cannot turn off sentences or chapters by the hour or the day, but only hesitatingly and more or less haltingly, as the mood seizes me, and only with such method, or lack of it, as the peculiar bent of my mind forces upon me. Neither am I, as probably the reader will easily realize, so "of imagination all compact" that I can throw myself, or seem to throw myself, with entire thoroughness into the past. The present weighs heavily upon my soul, and the future does not wear to me an aspect which sheds an especial light either upon the past or the present. I have, however, this excuse, possibly an insufficient one, for my discursiveness, that I am not pretending to write history but only a kind of autobiography;[1] not hoping to show, other than very partially and imperfectly, what Fenianism was and did, but only what I was to Fenianism, what I did or said at a certain period of my life, and what I now think of what I then said or did. All that may have no interest whatever for the world at large, and but a very faint one for that small fraction of it called Ireland, with which alone I greatly concern myself. I can only give what I have to give, and all this guessing at how the world, or my world, may take it, is probably very idle, though certainly a little natural.

But to come back from my meanderings to the pages of the *Irish People.* The thirty-ninth number of the

[1] And I am more or less troubled by the thought of a notion which has got abroad that I am doing the very thing which I am not, and that so many people, coming to my book, and not finding what they expected, will look with no favourable eye upon the far other thing which they will find. That, however, is unavoidable and inevitable, and, if possibly very much my misfortune, not at all my fault; anyway, I must console myself with the truism that "what will be, will be," or with that other one, that "what can't be cured must be endured."

second volume of the paper is cram-full of things Fenian or bearing on Fenianism, and its perusal would, I think, well repay the student[1] of that period, but the difficulty for me is to boil down the materials into such a compass as the space at my disposal will allow. As I have, however, but few other numbers to deal with, I shall dwell upon it at some length. The first two columns of our leading pages are taken up with "Answers to Correspondents," including much verse, which, if highly patriotic, is but faintly poetical. I give two short answers showing our troubles in two opposite directions. We could not always get the sort of aid we wanted, especially literary aid, from our friends, and we always met with unflinching opposition from the priests. Here is the first answer: "'Gerald' had better take to some other way of serving the cause. We are flooded with fervid but foolish verse in praise of the Fenians. It is easy to eulogize the Fenians, but to write poetry about them is another thing." The second "answer" is this: "'A correspondent' informs us that the Rev. Mr. O'Gorman, of Clogheen, has hunted down all there who, from time to time, became agents for the

[1] I am happy to have had unmistakable evidence lately that there are students, and very laborious, intelligent, and sympathetic ones too, of both the period and the paper. While I am writing these pages, I find a series of articles in the *Shamrock* on the "Literature of '67," by Mr. D. J. O'Donoghue, of London, the author of a very useful and exhaustive "Biographical Dictionary of Irish Poets." Mr. O'Donoghue is, of course, inevitably more or less inaccurate in mere matters of detail, but he is very full, and indeed very correct and well-informed, considering that he writes nearly entirely from materials already in print, without the possibility of any personal knowledge of the men or things of the time.

Irish People, and that after this week we are not to send any more copies unless some new agent turns up, able to act independently of this rev. gentleman." Neither of these answers need much (if any) comment now. Bad versifiers we have always amongst us; as I fear we shall always have priests opposed to all sound rational teaching. One thing I may however say. This direct interference with our agents was, I believe, the only part of the priests' action that was effective. They certainly succeeded in hindering or hampering the circulation of the paper in many places, and so imposed a financial loss upon us, as well as much worry, odium, and business injury upon many people. But they did not, so far as I could ever make out, succeed at all in stopping the spread of our ideas, save indeed to an almost inappreciable extent, and merely by mechanical means. So that, when shortly after the time to which I have now got, an end was made of us,—i.e. of the paper and its leading contributors,—as far as I can gather, an end was made of "priests in politics" too, at least for the time being. Our ideas survived our imprisonment, nor was action stopped by it, but only precipitated, and, anyway, such defeat as was inflicted upon us was due to the action of the English Government, not of the Irish priests. To be sure, the influence of the priests, if it did not survive, has revived with a vengeance, but that is a matter for present or future history, with which Fenianism, or my connection with it, has nothing to do, and I have no concern here with present politics, and no pretence whatever to any peculiar prophetic insight into the future.

The first of the leading articles is called " The Affray at Dangan," which was an affair in which a man was shot by the police; and we entirely deprecated all such disturbances, naturally objecting to such piecemeal fighting, under the worst possible conditions and at an altogether inopportune time. The second article is called " The Fenians," and deals scoffingly with some of the many ridiculous and mostly contradictory stories set afloat about them: "They are the terror alike of loyal Protestants and pious Catholics. They are denounced with equal gusto by Archbishop Cullen and the Rev. Tresham Gregg, by the 'National Association' and the Tory newspapers. Wrecking an Orange Lodge comes as easy to them as burning a priest in effigy; and these little exploits are of course intended partly to keep their hands in till the grand day arrives for cutting Protestant throats and hanging Catholic priests and bishops."

The writer of the article, who was, I think, Kickham, goes on to enumerate a number of ridiculous or wicked doings fathered upon the Fenians, by the papers, during the week, winding up with the alleged swearing-in of a " peeler," whose powers of invention appear to have been of the feeblest. We are told that " the peeler's name is Walsh. He has immortalized himself. He has been the first to bring what *must* be the true version of the Fenian oath—or at least a portion of it—to light. This respectable member of the Constabulary declareth upon oath that the 'Fenian' wanted him to swear allegiance *against the Queen of England and all her subjects.*"

The next article, headed " The Big Man of the West,"

is a long, elaborate, and amusing skit, by Luby, upon the sayings and doings, recorded by himself, of a certain Dr. Martin Andrew O'Brennan and several priests, at the Athlone election, which ended by inflicting upon that unfortunate and no doubt not over high-principled constituency a very objectionable London auctioneer of the name of Reardon.

Space will not allow me to give much of Luby's very good foolery. He had an easy and but too tempting victim in the ridiculous doctor: "He (the doctor) modestly says, 'We fled to lend our feeble aid to the electors of Athlone, that the world might see that they were not to be bought and sold like cattle.' Feeling that the eyes of an admiring world were upon them, he came resolved to conquer. The ignominy of Athlone no longer makes him feel 'his cheek crimsoned with the burning blush of shame.' He need 'sigh' over her fallen glories no more. To use his own expressive language—'The whole thing is a marvel.' 'Athlone is ransomed, its character redeemed, the stigma wiped out.'" And so on, with much more of the doctor's exaggerated and insincere rhetoric. Luby winds up his article with a short paragraph in which the badinage gradually gives way to sober seriousness. To quote from the *Battle of Aughrim*,[1] Athlone appears to be once more—

"'The pride of Empire and the throne of state.'

[1] This is a famous chap-book of the time, not unknown, I should think, to the present generation of Irishmen. It is a very queer production, written by a Protestant and a graduate of Trinity, and yet glorifying Sarsfield throughout. The line that goes before the one given by Luby is—

"Athlone is lost, that lovely *seat*."

Yet we doubt not that, in spite of the brilliant nature of Mr. Reardon's and Mr. O'Brennan's victory, cavillers will be found to say that the election was a farce from beginning to end, that all the actors in it were unmitigated humbugs, and that, if the men of Athlone desire to revive the historic fame of their town, it must be by actions like those of their fathers in the days of William the Third."

The last leading article—"Divide and Rule"—was my own. I go on to say that "certain Tory papers take some hasty words of Mr. Roberts, spoken at the Fenian pic-nic in New York, as the text for their declamation, and with characteristic unfairness make no mention of certain other words of the speech which more than modify the meaning of what they quote." These words of Mr. Roberts, modified or unmodified, or indeed anything said by that gentleman, make little difference to anyone at this distance of time. I merely allude to them here to explain the last paragraph of the article, which gives, I think, a fair view of the state of national opinion, as it unquestionably lays down the line of thought and action followed by us throughout. "The attempt to play the old game of divide and rule is but a bungling business this time. There is not the shadow of a reason for attributing narrow sectarian notions to any body of Nationalists at home or abroad. There are, to be sure,[1]

[1] I should say I must have been here alluding merely to the *Freeman's Journal*, the *Nation*, and the *Irish-American*, which were all three—but especially the last two—professedly National and Catholic, but to my mind very much more the last than the first. People may be a trifle puzzled by the mention of the *Nation* in this connection, but there have been *Nations* and *Nations*, and this was the *Nation* of the Messrs. Sullivan.

a few journals miscalled national, which still keep alive a spirit, if not of bigotry, at least of sectarianism. Happily, however, for the cause of Irish union, these journals have scarcely any influence on the National party. The same Tory papers which charge the Fenians with such fell designs against the peace of Protestants are in the habit of nick-naming this journal the 'Fenian organ,' but we defy them to point out one single line in its pages which could give just cause of offence to any Protestant or even to any well-meaning Orangeman.

'We hate the Saxon and the Dane,
We hate the Norman men—
We cursed their greed for blood and gain,
We curse them now again.
Yet start not, Irish-born man,
If you're to Ireland true,
We heed not blood, nor creed, nor clan,
We have no curse for you.

. . . . .

What matter that at different shrines
We pray unto one God—
What matter that at different times
Our fathers won this sod—
In fortune and in name we're bound
By stronger links than steel;
And neither can be safe nor sound
But in the other's weal.'"

There was no doubt about the creed of the Irish People, but, looking to some after-experience, and seeing the turn many things have taken since, I fear I was a little too sweeping in crediting all the people I chose to call Nationalists with the opinions of the *Irish People.* Still, I knew scarcely an exception then to the rule of unsectarianism among the so-called Fenians, and I have known very few since. But many things have gone back since both among the Irish at home and abroad, including the Fenians. The creed of Davis needs preaching again, and the creed must be the oftener heard because we cannot have it in the thundering tones of its original expounder.

In the same number of the paper we have some five columns of correspondence, nearly all occupying itself with the eternal "priests in politics" question, mostly taking very ugly shapes indeed, but perhaps the meanest and most usual form it took was the effort of the priests to deprive men of their means of living, merely because the said men thought differently from the said priests on political questions. A sufficiently ridiculous form we find clerical obstructionism taking is where a man is refused as sponsor for a child because he read the *Irish People.* The child was Con Keane's, then one of the Phœnix prisoners in Cork, and afterwards Fenian convict at Portland and elsewhere. Keane writes: "When I heard of the circumstance, I was not in the least surprised, neither was I vexed, as I believe the priest, who was the cause of one of the sponsors being refused, capable of committing any meanness. As to the sponsor who was refused, I believe him to be one of the most respectable young men in Skibbereen, and *the reason assigned by the priest for refusing him was that he read the 'Irish People.'*"

CHAPTER XXIV.

PRIESTS IN POLITICS, AND A PARTICULAR PRIEST.

TIMES have changed much in Ireland since those days, but most assuredly the priests have changed but little. For good or ill, they seem to be pretty much as they were, and perhaps, as I shall soon have done with the paper, priests, politics, and this book, this is as good a time as another to say a few words on our much-used and much-abused phrase—no priests in politics. Up to a short while ago, your orthodox agrarian person, with his P.P. as chairman of his society, and a C.C. as secretary, was quite ready to hold that the doctrine of "no priests in politics" was rank heresy. But agrarianists[1] have fallen out, the shoe pinches again, and one section is quite Fenian now on this "no priests in politics" question, while the other side, naturally, if not over wisely, thinks, or pretends to think, that there is flat blasphemy in the phrase.

[1] I use this awkward and ugly word for want of a better. It is easy to know what a Land League or a National League meant in relation to the land, but, *me judice*, mostly impossible to know what he meant in relation to Ireland. I cannot give these people either the good name of Nationalists or the bad one of Whigs, where I can but imperfectly know to what extent they deserve either epithet.

But what definitely did the phrase mean? Well, those who have followed me so far, and have seen what was written by us, or rather mostly by Kickham, ought not to have any great difficulty in the matter. We never meant to deny either to priest or to parson any of the ordinary rights of a citizen. He might, for aught we cared and certainly for aught we could help, speak, write, vote, and do all that any other man might. But that was all. When the priest and the priestly-minded took it upon themselves to think that priests should have a place in politics other than that of lawyers, doctors, carpenters, and other classes of citizens, then we entirely demurred. We also went a little farther, for we felt that, while there could be no question as to the rights of priests, there might be many as to their duties and the duty of others in their regard. We believed that priests generally had neither the political knowledge nor the political training which fitted them to guide others. We also no doubt thought, though I do not know that we ever particularly pressed the point, that there was one thing which altogether hampered a priest's action in politics, and should make the laity cautious in dealing with him. The priest is not a free agent. Behind him you have the bishop, behind the bishop the archbishop, and behind all these all kinds of elaborate and more or less occult machinery at Rome. You have to deal with all that and not with the individual priest. It would be easy to enlarge upon all this, but there is no need to do so here. To end these generalities —for I shall still have to deal with special priests and special actions of priests—we never denied to the priest his legitimate influence as a man, taking him for exactly what he was worth in that capacity, but we most emphatically denied that he should have any special influence as a priest; that, whenever and wherever he was allowed to have such an influence, he, being human (when not, like so many priests and laymen, quite inhuman), nearly always abused it.

This was, I think, roughly speaking, nearly all our contention, and if we were not, to a large extent (if not wholly) right in that, then I have read history to little purpose, and lived a long life in a world where all was dark to me.

In the issue of August 26th I find myself treating the question, if not of priests in politics, at least of a particular priest, in an article entitled "Father Maher on Fenians," which indeed might as well be called Father Maher on things in general and nothing in particular: "We print elsewhere a letter from a pen which used to be well known to the newspapers. We should scarcely have noticed Father Maher's lucubrations at all but for the fact that he is old and the uncle of Dr. Cullen. From the time of Nestor downwards, old age is supposed to confer a sort of long-winded sagacity, and so near and venerable a relative must be supposed, in some degree, to share the counsels of the ecclesiastically all-potent Archbishop. "Father Maher," I go on to say, "holds out a certain candidate for the Queen's County as a frightful example of Fenianism, which he certainly neither is, nor by any possibility could be. The redoubtable Captain or Mr. McDonnell, went in, we understand, mainly on what may be called the parish priest interest, and relied for his return on some half-dozen clerical cousins and a little hard cash.[1] To be sure, the unfortunate man reckoned slightly without his host, and did not take proper account of the parish priests who were not his relatives. At any rate, the sayings and doings of extraneous McDonnells are no business of ours, and we think it would be very much more to the purpose if the parish priest of Graigue pitched into his brother parish priests. Electioneering humbug may prove much against Father Maher, but it can't prove anything against the Fenian Brotherhood or its friends." I then quote a passage which in its undiluted O'Connellism may be a sort of curiosity at the present day: "The leading principles of that peaceful agitation by which Ireland gained a large instalment of her rights was thus expressed by O'Connell, 'Liberty was too dearly bought by the shedding of human blood,'[2] and that 'whoever committed crime or violated the law was an enemy of his country.'

. . . . . .

[1] Of course, at this distance of time, I cannot know whether my information as to the Captain, save in regard to his non-Fenianism, was absolutely correct, but the man is a mere name to me, while the thing—priests favouring nephews, cousins, and the like—was then, and is still, of common occurrence.

[2] The supposed O'Connell saying, which, by the way, I have no convenient means of verifying, is somewhat watered down here. What used to be attributed to him was that "No political amelioration is worth the shedding of one drop of blood;" a doctrine of which it is hard to say whether it is the more foolish or the more base. But there is the probable excuse for O'Connell, that, when he talked such trash, his brain was softening.

"What has been gained in America by the horrible butchery, these last four years, of more than a million of her bravest sons? What in Naples or Sicily? What in Paris of the slaughter of 40,000 men in the memorable days of July? Playing at soldiers in civil war is always a losing game on both sides." The article proceeds to say: "We suppose that Father Maher means the memorable days of June; but we will not quarrel with his history. If an archbishop may mistake Gustavus Adolphus for Gustavus Vasa, why should not meaner men be allowed to make their little slips too? Playing at war is certainly a losing game, but seems a strange phrase to apply to one of the greatest struggles of modern times. If we rightly understand Father Maher, he thinks war a purely Pagan idea, and, if so, we should like to know what he thinks of the Pope in his political capacity."

It seems as if Father Maher had infected me with a little of his own verbosity, for I find that this article of mine runs to the unusual (for me) length of a column and a quarter, largely, however, made up of extracts from the long-winded P.P. himself. I shall, however, inflict but little more either of Father Maher or myself upon the reader. I say: "It is hard to pick out the points of Father Maher's long letter. Fenianism, as presented to him by Captain McDonnell and his own imagination, is his grand theme, but he does not forget to lash his old enemy, Young Irelandism, also. The Fenians are, he thinks, the lawful offspring of the Young Irelanders. And so, in principle, they are, as both are the legitimate descendants of the 'miscreants of '98.'[1] It was the Young Irelanders who broke up O'Connell's great agitating machine, though some of them set up[2] little ones of their own to-day. It was the Young Irelanders who first separated priests and people in politics. We are not sorry that Father Maher reminds them of these facts, for some of them have very short memories. One of them cannot even remember that he was not a young man in '48." I then give a long passage from Father Maher upon evictions, extermination, depopulation, and the like; but, as all that had about as little to do with Fenianism as Fenianism with it, my comment is of the shortest: "Such are our ills, but how are they to be cured? Why, by the old familiar process of petitioning, of course. Father Maher is probably not a modest man; but we would ask him if he, by one effort, expects to do more than twenty-four bishops and countless priests by their united energies have done in eight months?"

[1] One of the many unhappy phrases attributed to O'Connell.

[2] I must be here alluding to the Association got up by Archbishop Cullen, John Dillon, and others. But it matters little. That body, as far as I could hear, never did anything, nor did any other agitating body, till the mind of Mr. Gladstone was awakened by the blowing down of a piece of wall or something else; anyway, it most assuredly was not awakened by the eloquence of Archbishop Cullen, John Dillon, and the others.

CHAPTER XXV.

TWO HEROIC NATIONS.

THE most important article in this number was the last, and is by Luby. As was usual with him, it is long, and for that as for other reasons I can give but an imperfect account of it. The article is called "Two Heroic Nations," and here is the opening paragraph, the moral of which is as sound now as the day it was written :—" Brave nations never despair. After the greatest disasters they rally. Struck down by tyranny again and again, they invariably seize the earliest opportunity of renewing resistance. Nor are these efforts for ever unavailing. A day comes at last when their heroic perseverance finds its reward. Sooner or later, they are sure to be crowned with either partial or complete success. At worst, those who combat opposition with unyielding valour, are certain, in the long run, to get better terms than submissive dastards." Here is some of what Luby says about that one of his two brave nations to which the main portion of his article is devoted: "From the first moment the Anglo-Saxon strangers set foot on their shores, the aborigines of New Zealand, like ourselves, have seldom ceased to defend themselves against foreign encroachment. Inch by inch they have disputed the possession of their native isles with the invaders. In their most evil days they were never hopelessly vanquished. These oppressors in their arrogance call them a race of savages. But, if they be indeed savages, no other savages have ever displayed such ingenuity, bravery, energy, and elasticity of spirit. Though a mere handful (the British settlers alone, without mentioning the regular British troops, are said to be numerically superior to the natives), they gained all they demanded in the last New Zealand War, compelling the English to admit themselves in the wrong. In the present war they have more than once humbled the flag of England, and now the latest accounts inform us 'that affairs have come to a deadlock.'"

Luby then goes into a long account, which I cannot follow here, of men and things in New Zealand, and the Colonial Office, and the English Press. Things have changed since, and there has been no Maori war quite lately, and perhaps there may never be another. It may be, too, that the Maori race is destined to extinction, but it will not die out the sooner because brave men died for it, and let us hope that it may not die out at all. This dying out of the savage before the civilized, or of the primitive before the sophisticated, is an ugly moral problem with which I have no very direct business here. I jump to the last paragraph of Luby's article, where he treats of his second brave nation, and here we have a case which, if not in itself more interesting than that of the Maoris, is certainly far more important, and comes much more home to our own "business and bosom":—

"A word, ere we conclude, about another brave nation, that, though long pursued 'by unmerciful disaster,' never despairs of its future. This nation occupies a far larger space in the world's eye than the small primitive tribes of New Zealand. It belongs to one of the races of the great Caucasian family of mankind. Its history is, in many respects, glorious. On one occasion, at least, it was the military pride and prop of Christendom and civilization. We allude, of course, to heroic Poland. Our last number contained an account of the reception given by the citizens of Lugano, in Switzerland, to General Langievicz, ex-Dictator of Poland. They presented him with an address expressing their sympathies with the cause of Poland. The General's reply shows that he has not ceased to hope that one day Poland will be free. He says his 'hope is not an illusion.' He even draws encouragement from Poland's recent defeat. He says, 'During eighteen months some warriors, unselected, clothed in rags, half fed, half armed, held out against the armies of a colossal monarchy, supported by two powerful empires which for a century took part in a great crime.' He shows how divisions were sown in the Polish ranks, and how aristocratic pride and ambition prevented the war being made a popular one. Who can refuse to believe that, if, with proper resources, the united Polish people had flung themselves into the struggle as one man, a glorious triumph would have restored Poland to her rank among the nations? Poland will never despair of herself. No subject country *should* ever despair or 'give in.' Where freedom is the glorious prize, a people, beaten again and again, should again and again renew the fight."

Bating a certain temperamental sanguineness in the general tone and in some questions of detail, this is as true to-day as when it was written. Your common-sensical wiseacre will, of course, tell me, as if he were inspired and I were an idiot, that one country cannot fight three, nor a very small one a very big one. Let us concede, for the sake of argument, so much to common sense; but may not the three countries fall out, or the big one grow small or the small one bigger, or the small one get the aid of one big one against another? But all this, *pace* our common-sensical friend, is not, and never was, a mere question of counting of heads, but rather of counting of hearts. If the wiseacres were only sincere or consistent, what fools they must take the "three hundred men and three men" to have been! Indeed, I was told but the other day by one of these, a highly-educated, advanced (socialistic in fact) English gentleman, that Stephens was a fool and Wolfe Tone ditto. Well, no doubt there is a sense in which they were, as there is a sense in which we talk of the folly of the cross.

CHAPTER XXVI.

VARIOUS CONTRIBUTORS AND VARIOUS CONTRIBUTIONS.

IN this paper there are nearly nine columns of correspondence, of course largely devoted to priests in general, and on this occasion occupying itself considerably with Father Maher in particular. Here too I find the first and last contribution of my old friend "Eva," of the *Nation.* Before she could write again there was an end of the paper, and total and protracted eclipse of ourselves.

In the next number of the paper, which is the last but two, I find myself, curiously enough, unable to say, with any degree of definiteness, who wrote any of the articles. Three out of four of these are taken up with comments upon the notions of various English publications—*Fraser's Magazine*, the *Times*, the *Telegraph*, etc.—on Ireland. In one of the articles entitled "English Estimate of Irish Intellect," Archbishop Whately is quoted as saying that the English have for ages treated the Irish as the Lord Chancellor treats a lunatic—as people unfitted to be entrusted with the management of their own affairs.[1]

[1] The English, or at least a portion of them, have of late mended their hands a little in this matter. They are now for

One long passage I may give from this article, which I think gives briefly and forcibly a summary of the dealings of England with this country: "It is not, however, governmental functions only for which Irishmen are deemed unsuited by English arrogance. We are, in the estimate of our rulers, equally unqualified for the vulgar pursuits of industry. Owing to our incurable incapacity, the English found themselves obliged to suppress our woollen trade by Act of Parliament—to close our ports against foreign commerce, and even to prohibit the exportation of Irish cattle to English markets. Our dulness, our stupidity, our incapacity for trade induced the English to have recourse to those prohibitive measures. We are 'children' whom they have endeavoured to instruct by establishing among us, by law, a Church of English origin and an Orange Society, which likewise originated in England.[2] This was done with the most benevolent intentions, though ungrateful Irishmen are blind to the efforts which Englishmen have repeatedly made to civilize them. With the view of civilizing us—as their historians have told us—Henry II. invaded this country, with Adrian's

entrusting us with the management of some part of our affairs; but how much, I think it passes the art of man to make out, as most certainly it passes mine.

[2] I do not know what is the authority of the writer, whom I suspect to be O'Keeffe, for this statement. As this is the first mention of O'Keeffe (who wrote much for us), and may be the last, I had better perhaps say a word or two about him. He wrote forcibly, if without any great distinction in thought or in style, and with considerable knowledge of things Irish and other; but he was half cracked, his strongest craze being that you could make Ulster men Nationalist, and so secure the freedom of Ireland, by getting the Irish in America to Boycott Belfast linen.

Bull[1] in his girdle, to civilize us. Elizabeth strewed the island with carcasses and ashes. Cromwell butchered us with the same humane views, and William III. confiscated our estates with the hope of 'improving the right owners.'

> 'The Irish had long made a deuce of a clatter,
> And wrangled and fought about *meum* and *tuum*,
> Till England stept in and decided the matter,
> By kindly converting it all into *suum*.'

"Rejoicing at the extermination of our peasantry the *Times* the other day said, 'The Celt goes to yield the soil to the Saxon. The island of 160 harbours, with a fertile soil, with noble rivers and beautiful lakes, with fertile mines and riches of every kind, is being cleared away quietly for the necessities and luxuries of *humanity*.' From this it appears that Irishmen are not human beings."

If there was no word in our leading columns this week on the "priests in politics question," it crops up more than once in our correspondence department, where I find myself, in answer to a correspondent, laying down our position briefly: "We willingly give the foregoing letter," one, which, while expressing general agreement with our views, takes exception to the letters of our correspondents about the priests, "though it is a perfect mystery to us why such letters are ever written. We cannot form the faintest conception of how the notion gets into the heads

[1] The existence of this bull has been denied by many ecclesiastics, notably by Cardinal Moran, but most people still believe in its authenticity.

of well-meaning men that we go out of our way to attack the priests. The priests invariably attack us first, and it is not the priest but the politician we care to censure."

In the next number of the paper I have to deal with another letter-writer, to whom I say:—"We cannot for the life of us see the harm of the letters condemned by Mr. Murphy, or what they have in common with the writings of Voltaire. Is it infidelity to criticize the conduct of priests as politicians? Will Mr. Murphy say what he disapproves of?" I may also ask now, does anybody believe that Kickham, who was the chief critic of the priests, was an infidel? But the whole matter, to my mind, lies in a nutshell. The priests then, as now, simply held that they were above criticism whereas it would be much nearer the truth to say that they were below it. And then, as now, there were plenty of weak-minded people who thought (if one can speak of thought in such a connection) that you had no *right* to censure a priest for his political sins or shortcomings, because by so doing you lessened his legitimate spiritual influence. But when did this injury come in? Did it not all come from the fact that the priest used, or rather abused, his spiritual influence for mere political, and very often for grossly material and unspiritual, ends. Let us freely grant, what cannot be denied by anyone who knows history, Irish or other, that in this quarrel, infidels, or at least non-Catholics, are constantly made. But who makes them? Undoubtedly, the priest in politics. It is of course not logical that a man should cease to be a

Catholic because or in consequence of a priest doing as he should not; but then most men are not logical, and priests are quite as little logical as other men. It is the situation which is mainly in fault. Given a set of men who have some sort of notion that they have some sort of divine right to stuff their opinions down other people's throats, and people silly or weak enough to let their throats be crammed, and all the rest flows naturally from that. Those who are not silly or weak must hold that such so-called right is a clear wrong, and so of diabolic rather than divine origin. But why pursue this theme? It is an endless one. Priests we have always among us—and fools are little likely to fail us. But happily some sprinkling we always have also of the wise (or comparatively wise) and the strong (or comparatively strong), and 'tis their views that prevail in the long run.

I have now reached the last number but one of the paper, and as I have been having, even on the priests in politics question, most of the talk to myself, I can the easier cease to be vocal on that theme, as I find that Kickham treats his usual subject in the last number of all. In this paper (Sept. 9th), we have a phenomenally lengthy and somewhat belated article by Luby. It is about three columns long, was crushed out of the previous number, and deals with the sayings and doings, or rather misdoings, of John Francis Maguire, then, and in a measure, I should say, still, well known to the Irish public. But, as the man is now long since dead, and represents little that is going on in the world around us, and was no worse if no better than the ruck of politicians who went before or came after him, I may as well let them "rest in the shade."

Luby only leaves room for less than two columns of leading matter, and one of these is used by me to deal with the notions of the newspapers, especially the *Times*, about the Fenians. "It is the almost universal belief (if people mean what they say) of the newspapers, English and Irish, that the Fenians are fools. To be sure, the papers do not seem to know what they are, or whether they are at all, but, if they are, they are certainly fools. We are supposed to know these Fenians well, though we have, over and over again, disclaimed all knowledge of them. We invariably mean what we say, and so unfortunately (or fortunately) it must be our lot to be mistaken, not to say misrepresented, by a certain section of the community. We certainly know a good deal about the Fenian Brotherhood in America, and must be allowed to consider that body anything but a foolish one. We shall, however, make this concession to public opinion, that the Fenians, in the newspapers, are, if not fools, at least bores, and threaten to become positive nuisances." The article then goes on to cull certain elegant extracts from an article of the *Times*, the whole of which is given in another part of the paper. Here is some of the fun poked at us by the *Times*: "Many Irishmen have of late taken to a new kind of nocturnal amusement. They meet on the roads, or on any dry bit of ground they can find, and go through what they consider to be drilling, and what no doubt is drilling. . . . Then, if it be really drilling, and if these men are learning the trade of soldiering, why not? They do it *gratis*, and without the actual use of dangerous edged tools. A good many of them will finish by taking the Queen's shilling and fighting, as Irishmen always do fight, against Her Majesty's enemies."[1]

I find it neither easy nor necessary to hitch in my comment here, but pass on from the sorry fun of the *Times* to its sad earnest. It seems to have realized the fact that all the fighting would not be against the Queen's enemies: "We will not speculate as to the result of the supposed campaign; nor is it necessary, for in any result, whether success or failure, the Americans would eventually withdraw their forces from Ireland and leave its excited population to our own tender mercies. We trust that in that dark hour the counsels of mercy would prevail, and that England would interfere to assuage the fury of factions, and even to soften the avenger of blood. But there is such a thing as martial law, and there have been some commanders apt to give a free vent to their sense of indignation and their hatred of treason. There are men in this country we should be sorry, indeed, to let loose upon Ireland, even should

[1] There was another side to all that, not then known to the *Times*, but since well-known from the Fenian trials. Irishmen certainly but too often take the "Saxon Shilling," but it is only the veriest of *gobemouches* that believes that this is from any love of the Saxon or the Saxon Queen. They fight her enemies! Yes, but they would far sooner fight her friends, on the side of her enemies. As I have said more than once in this book, 'twas easier to make a Fenian of a soldier than of almost any man. Of course it was immoral to swear allegiance to the English Queen, and then to the Irish Republic, but I must be excused for holding that the immorality lay rather in the first than in the last.

Ireland itself lack at that crisis an adequate representative of British loyalty and Orange predilections." To all of which my answer was simply this: "We all remember the Indian Mutiny, and most of us read the English newspapers of the time, and few of us will be at any loss to make out what all this means. But we are men, not children, and the *Times* may keep its thunder for timider temperaments." I might have added that we, who feared not to speak of '98, knew but too well what England's tender mercies had been then!

CHAPTER XXVII.

OUR LAST NUMBER.

THE last number of the paper is dated the 16th of September, 1865, and there is nothing particularly explosive or indeed anyway phenomenal about it. We had no "Jacta alea est," "Tocsin of Ireland,"[1] or other rhetorical fireworks. We did not know we were at our last gasp, and so could prepare no fitting dying phrases. Indeed, I do not think that we were ever much given to the making of phrases; but on that matter the reader of this book ought by this time to be able to judge for himself.

The opening article, by Kickham, is on the never-ending theme, and some of this I must give, as explaining and summarizing the position we held all along: "Nothing would please us better than to keep clear of the vexed question of priests in politics if we could do so without injury to the cause which we were endeavouring to serve. But the question was forced upon us. We saw clearly that the people should be taught to distinguish between the priest as a minister of religion

[1] Titles of very eloquent and inflammatory articles in the suppressed number of the *Nation*.

and the priest as a politician before they could be got to advance one step on the road to independence. . . . Our only hope is in revolution. But most of the bishops and many of the clergy are opposed to revolution. Is it not then the duty of the Irish patriot, be he priest or layman, to teach the people that they have a right to judge for themselves in temporal matters? This is what we have done. We have over and over declared it was our wish that people should respect and be guided by their clergy in spiritual matters.[1] But when priests turn the altar into a platform; when it is pronounced a 'mortal sin' to read the *Irish People*, a 'mortal sin' even to *wish* that Ireland should be free; when priests actually call upon the people to turn informers, and openly threaten to set the police upon the track of men who are labouring in the cause for which our fathers so often bled; when true men are reviled and slandered; when the up-rooting of the people is called a 'merciful dispensation of Providence'; when, in a word, bishops and priests are doing the work of the enemy—we believe it is our duty to tell the people that

[1] I think Kickham is somewhat over-stating the case here. He may himself have done this, and more than once, but it was no business of the paper to tell the people how they should be guided in spiritual matters. I had myself laid down our position definitely in the previous number of the paper. Here is what I said: "We cannot allow our correspondent to carry off the notion that this journal is a Catholic one. It is neither Catholic nor Protestant, but simply Irish. Catholics and Protestants serve Ireland in its columns as in the ranks of the National party." Of course, we were always strong for all things spiritual as opposed to things merely material, for setting the soul above the stomach, but as to how people should shape their religious beliefs, that was no concern of ours.

the bishops and priests may be bad politicians and worse Irishmen."

The article, in a long paragraph, goes on to say how, before our paper was in being, the bishops had condemned "dangerous brotherhoods," whether oath-bound or not; and how the "Brotherhood of St. Patrick" and the "Fenian Brotherhood," though not oath-bound, by no means escaped the censure of certain ecclesiastics. The paragraph winds up with the following passage: "We have never written a word calculated to injure religion in the slightest degree. We challenge our assailants to point to a single sentence in the *Irish People*, from its first number to its present, which could be construed into an attack upon religion. The charge that we are enemies of the Catholic Church is a vile calumny invented by trading politicians, and perhaps believed by weak men who are ready to believe anything of anyone who would dare to question their right to dictate to the people, or to disturb the peaceful contentment of their lives."

Such were some of the principal contentions of Kickham at the time, and now, after a generation, I fail to see that there was almost anything in what he said which was not very much to the purpose. He winds up his article by saying that, "After all, the war we have been forced to wage against ecclesiastical dictation in politics has done some good. The people are now so used to denunciation, there is no reason to fear they will be frightened by it when the time has come for the final struggle. This is something to be thankful for."

Here Kickham certainly does not over-state or over-estimate what we, and especially what he, had done. There was very much to be thankful for, though the thing could not be put to the test of that "final struggle"—which never came. In such spasmodic and intermittent *struggles* as did take place, however, I cannot make out that the priest counted for anything, one way or the other. Now you have a "struggle" of another sort, to what extent final or not, time alone can tell, and in this the priests unfortunately count for much. But that was no fault of Kickham or myself, and it is no present business of mine—especially in these pages—to tell how the priests came back to power, what is the extent of that power, or what should be done to diminish or destroy a power, *me judice*, mostly ill-got, and almost invariably ill-used.

Kickham is followed in this last number by a long and amusing article on "The Fenians and the Fairies," by I know not whom, memory playing one of her strange tricks upon me here again. The last article—"The Sister Islands"—seems to be by myself, and is mostly devoted to ridicule of the people who held, or pretended to hold, that we were growing fonder of England; precursors of the union of hearts fools and rogues, with the difference in their favour that they did not claim to be Nationalists of any kind. In the last paragraph, I (if it be I) drop joking and come to more or less grim earnest; grim at least it seems to me now, seeing what so soon followed it then. "Those who still persist in putting faith in Irish loyalty will, no doubt, be inclined to call the British Government both irrational and tyrannical. No doubt, if the Irish be really as loyal as the advocates of British connection would fain persuade the world they are, the conduct of English rulers is at once stupid and inhuman. But as we cannot help feeling more than sceptical about Irish loyalty, as we believe the masses of our countrymen as little ultra-loyal as we are ourselves, we cannot consistently complain, however much we may sympathize with the people, that England won't let us have Volunteers or allow us to practise drilling. Neither can we reasonably expect to get fair trials in her courts. England's conduct, under all the circumstances of the case, seems quite natural. If Irishmen want to be citizen-soldiers, if they wish for an impartial administration of justice—it appears to us that they must look to themselves, and not to English rulers, for these great privileges."

In another part of the paper—the "Answers to Correspondents"—which was more especially my own ground, I dealt with a matter upon which our English instructors are for ever crediting or discrediting us with opinions which few if any of us have:—

"We give elsewhere, from the *Pall Mall Gazette*, a specimen of the astounding articles with which the English have been favouring us of late. Perhaps the queerest part of this article is the talk about Saxons and Celts. We need scarcely tell our readers that we know no difference between Saxons and Celts in Ireland. Many of us do not know whether we are Saxons or Celts, and most of us do not know how much Saxon or

Celtic blood may be in our veins. In fact we care nothing from what part of the world, or at what period of its history, a man's ancestors came to Ireland. The *Pall Mall Gazette* is, however, right in one point, and that is, that the people care very little for the abolition of the Church Establishment. By-the-bye, it is strangely suggestive that papers like the *Times* and *Pall Mall Gazette*, and papers like the *Nation* and *Universal News*, should be of one mind about the Fenians."

I do not know that I need say much more about this last number. There was a good literary article—"Infantry and Cavalry"—by "Ollamh Fodhla," whom I take to be O'Keeffe; poems by "Kilmartin" (John Walsh) and Cliodhna (Mrs. O'Donovan); and the usual quantity of correspondence.

As the reader may perceive, there was nothing particularly explosive in the paper, and of course its suppression was in no sense motived by its contents. We began perhaps somewhat spasmodically, at least in so far as the first article in the three first numbers could give a tone to the paper, we went on, I hope, forcibly, and we ended very quietly indeed, so far as this mere side of things was concerned. To be sure, there was a far other side of things, with which some of us were now to become unpleasantly acquainted, and of which I shall say something before I end.

Meanwhile, I have done with the paper. I hope I have in this long perambulation through its pages made myself (or rather my matter) fairly interesting to the reader. I know I have been intelligible, which is something, but it is one of the hardest things in life for me to know what aspect our thoughts, or the colour we gave them, will wear in the eyes of Irishmen of this generation. What we wrote, in those now distant days, was certainly not without a strong influence upon our own generation, and to me, knowing at least that, and trying to live those old times over again, and with that natural leaning of the old towards the time past, and especially towards one's own past, I feel as if I may have easily lent an air of bigness and breadth to things more or less small and narrow. I know not. "What do I know?" ("Que sais-je?") as says wise Montaigne. *Litera scripta manet*, and I must only console myself with the thought that I have done as best I could under somewhat difficult circumstances, and leave the rest to that Fate which is, happily, for ever dark to all of us.

CHAPTER XXVIII.

ARREST, IMPRISONMENT AND TRIAL.

I MEANT to have ended my story with the account of my arrest, but I have been told that my imprisonment before conviction and the trials—at least Luby's and my own—come fairly within my recollections of the old Fenianism; and I must grant that they do, and that some treatment of this short period and of these simple events is needed, to give anything like completeness to a narrative which will be, I fear, at best but incomplete enough.

I set about my supplementary task, then, with such good will as I have got, but with little heart in it. It is years since I added anything to the book which is running through the press as I write, and the bother and worry of reading and re-reading what has been so long written and so often read, leaves me so little satisfied with what I have already said that I hardly know how to say any more just now.

However, to come to the beginning of the end, speaking, as our English friends may possibly think, somewhat Hibernically. On the night of the 14th of September, 1865, a raid was made on the office of the *Irish People*, all in it seized, and certain people in or about the office arrested, some at the time of the seizure, and some (notably, I believe, Rossa) as they came into or about the place shortly after. All this took place about nine o'clock, and was unknown to me till some hours later, when, after returning from the theatre and leaving a lady friend of mine (in fact, the sister of "Eva," of the *Nation*) at her lodgings, I returned home and quite unsuspectingly let myself in to my own lodgings, and, almost literally, into the arms of the detectives, two confronting me in the hall and two others pushing their way quietly in behind me. This was certainly a surprise to me, though scarcely anything very surprising in itself. Nor were there wanting certain elements of the comic in a situation sufficiently serious in itself. I remember that about the first thing I did, after getting in, was to seat myself comfortably in an arm-chair, requesting my captors to wait, which they politely and patiently did, while I smoked a pipe and flavoured it with a glass of whisky and water.

And this may be as good a place as any other to mention two matters, one favourable and the other unfavourable to official men and methods. During all the time of our imprisonment, previous to conviction, we found the police invariably civil and courteous, and, so far as one could at all judge from superficial signs, even sympathetic. The second matter has reference to that habit of smoking, which, if it wore a comic aspect in that slight incident mentioned above, soon after became to me the source of the most horrible discomfort, amounting at first to something like absolute pain. When we were shut up in Richmond prison, I found myself at once forced to lay down my pipe, with the result upon my nervous system of intense depression of spirits during the day and great sleeplessness at night, both continuing for how long a period I cannot now say. I of course protested against what was (to me) a very severe form of punishment, while merely accused of having done something which the powers that were supposed to deserve punishment, but I was quite powerless against "red tape." This may seem to be, and to actually be, a very small matter, quite beneath the dignity of history; but, as I have said over and over again, I am not writing history, but certain things relating to myself, or relating me to other persons and things, and the matter was anything but small to me at the time, and seems still to me a good example of the headlessness, not to say heartlessness, of official men and methods.

But I am anticipating, and, as usual, digressing. I am not as yet at Richmond, though fast on my way there. I am at first taken by my still considerate captors, or by this time rather custodians, to some police station—Chancery Lane, I think—but whether that or another matters nothing. Here, after some formalities on the part of some superior policeman, I am soon consigned to a cell, in company with two others, presumably Fenians, though neither of them was convicted. One of them was a queer fellow, and some sort of a city bagman in a small way, of whom I shall have one thing rather amusing to tell further on. The other was a young man of the name of Roantree, brother of a well-known member of the organization, whom I have mentioned before as succeeding Devoy in the charge of the soldiers. There was nothing queer about young Roantree, but, on the contrary, everything that was eminently respectable, and, I should say—knowing little, then or since, but the look and name of him—somewhat commonplace. I am perhaps digressing again, but these two young men have a sort of interest for me, though, as far as I know, having none in themselves, from my having spent in their company a very memorable, if anything but comfortable or comforting, night and morning!

The next morning we were brought up before a police magistrate of the name of Strong. There were, I fancy, about a dozen of us, but who these were (Luby and Rossa were certainly among them, and so were, I feel pretty confident, James O'Connor and George Hoppen also), or what was their exact number, I know not, nor have I either time or inclination, just now, to fish up numbers or names out of the files of old newspapers. I feel as if I were allowing these preliminary incidents, slight in themselves, though doubtless looming large in my eyes at the time, to delay me too long on my way to the last scene of all—the trials! but I shall glide quickly over this police court business, save that I must dwell at some length upon one part of it, which has still much interest for me, and with which my name has all along been much mixed up, though rather as accuser than as accused. Now, for the first time, I think, commenced a series of infamously calumnious charges against the Fenians, which, though ever varying in form and shifting in time, have gone on down to the very time (May, 1896) I am writing, and no doubt will go on long after there is an end of this book and of its author. But to come to this matter, which must necessarily crop up again upon my trial. Mr. Barry, then Law Adviser to the Castle, but long since a very well-known and, I understand, very distinguished Lord Justice, not content with merely setting forth (or at least those who briefed him not being content that he should merely set forth) such proofs as he could supply to secure our committal for treasonable practices, chose (or was made to choose), in addition, to accuse us of the intention to commit nearly all the crimes of the calendar—wholesale robbery, incendiarism, murder, and what not—and all this without one tittle of evidence for these charges, either then or after, and without one word of explanation or any withdrawal of the charges, until the time, some months after, of our trials, when they were implicitly, though not explicitly, withdrawn by the fact that nothing whatever was said about them.[1] Little need be added to what is

[1] I have put in these awkward parenthetic qualifying clauses above, because I have been told, by a distinguished lawyer friend of mine, that I was unfair to Mr. Barry, inasmuch as he was justified, by legal etiquette and ethics, I suppose, in putting forward what was set down for him in his brief, and which he must always assume can be proved. This may be so, but is a sort of morality, nevertheless, not clear to the non-legal mind, and certainly no inkling of it had dawned upon my mind when, on my trial, I denounced Mr. Barry as a moral assassin. It must be remembered that these calumnies were let go quite uncontradicted for months, in the meantime inflaming the public mind, necessarily including the mind of jurors.

said in the note below about this preliminary police inquiry.

And here I feel as if I ought to say a few words upon a kindred subject, though not coming properly within the range of these recollections. The Phœnix Park murders have been set down, even up to the time I write, by numberless literary *gobemouches* and designing political rogues, as Fenian crimes, but I deliberately assert that the thing was from beginning to end a crime arising out of the Land League. Two individuals, whose names I do not give, but who fled the country (scarcely for their country's good, for they have done her even greater evil since they fled) shortly after the commission of the crime, have been more than suspected of having hatched this horrible plot. But it is no case of strong suspicion, but one of absolute certainty, against some other prominent members of the Land League, for Mr. Frank Byrne, secretary to the Land League in England, Mr. John Walshe, organizer to the League in the North of England, and Mr. P. J. Sheridan, organizer for Connaught, have, one and all, not only acknowledged, but gloried in their complicity in this crime. Granted that all these men had been Fenians. They were not then acting as Fenians, but, as they well knew, dead in the teeth of what any responsible Fenian would in the least countenance; in fact, as Kickham said at the time, truly and felicitously (before he had learned any of the details), they were, if Fenians, "Fenians seduced by the Land League." Though I have necessarily gone into this matter but slightly and shortly, I think I have said enough.

I cannot of course in the least close the mouths of the literary *gobemouches*, but I think I may do something to teach the designing political knaves that it is not quite so safe, as so many of them have apparently thought, to try to saddle their own and their friends' crime on the shoulders of their enemies and the enemies of all crime, other than what Englishmen naturally consider crime, but all true Irishmen esteem as the highest virtue—High Treason.

Certain documents were of course read, including, I believe, a letter of that half-cracked O'Keeffe of whom I have said something before, upon which alone was based that tall column of fiction raised by Mr. Barry. The only oral evidence given was by a man of the name of Nagle, an ex-National teacher, for some time employed as a folder of papers in the office of the *Irish People*, but since well-known in the annals of infamy. I mention this man's name here, mainly to state that, on this his first public appearance, he swore I was a Fenian—which I certainly was, some lady in Belfast notwithstanding; but then this creature could know nothing about it, personally knowing nothing about me, save that I was constantly in the office of the paper, and, as he swore at my trial, supposed to be its editor. We were, of course, committed on the charge of treason-felony, without much protest on our part, though not, as well as I remember, without much aimless orating on all sides. Some short time after we were brought into the prison yard (Richmond), and there told that the indictment against us had been changed to one for high treason. And here comes in the somewhat comic, or at least grotesque, story about my queer companion of the police cell. When we had been told of the change in the *venue*, and before we could disperse, my commercial friend, to the intense amusement of all, cried out from our ranks, "High thrayson, bedad," evidently being much more impressed with the seemingly dignified position in which he stood than any way apprehensive of the possibly unpleasant consequences it might entail. The commercial man's neck was happily in no danger, nor do I remember that I thought at the time that any of our necks were in any very great danger, though I see, in looking into something written by Rossa for an American paper several years ago, that he "actually hanged himself in imagination that day, preparing himself for the worst." Rossa was scarcely more nervous than I was, but he was apparently very much more imaginative. But enough about hanging. Too many people in Ireland are always hanging themselves and others in imagination, and far too few, of late years at least, show any very strong inclination to put themselves in the way of realizing their imaginings.

Of the months spent in prison, before trial, I cannot feel as if it were necessary to say much, though much I remember about them, and many things of more or less interest occurred, and during all the time I was in a state of intense anxiety, not so much, I think, about our impending trials, as about the progress and prospects of the conspiracy. And this reminds me of the event, first in importance though not in time, which occurred during our detention before trial. This was the Convention from time to time, to some good-humoured chaff from Butt. Butt, as the leader on my side, replied to Lawson, and, of course, spoke ably and effectively, but I remember distinctly that his speech did not quite, if indeed at all, come up to my measure of the man, or what I expected from him. Of course, in all this I am merely giving my "recollections" of what I thought at the time, and not, by the reading of the very lengthy proceedings on the trial, seeking to form any judgment in the present. In the case of Luby there was only one speech for the prosecution, and one for the defence, for his *guilt*, in the eye of English law or of any juror who regarded it, was but too evident, while in my case the thing looked certainly different to myself, and presumably so to the lawyers on both sides, and so I was honoured, as I was certainly interested and amused, by two speeches in prosecution and two in defence. The Solicitor-General, Sullivan, replied to Butt, and did his business in what I took to be a very able and effective manner, but the best of all the speeches, to my mind, was the last on my side, which was delivered by Dowse, afterwards well-known in the English House of Commons and on the Irish Bench. Dowse had been a Young Irelander and a contributor to National journals in his youthful days, and possibly may have had some leaven of the old feeling left in him, though I incline to think that what he said so well with his broad Northern brogue was rather the outcome of his head than of his heart. Then, or at least after some technical intervening proceedings upon which I do not care to touch, came what I thought at the time the ablest speech against me. This was the charge of the judge, Mr. Justice Fitzgerald, who, feeling that the case against me was not strong (there was, for instance, no direct proof whatever that I was a Fenian), or at least was very weak compared to that against Luby (in which Keogh could afford to be quite judicial), took upon himself the *rôle* of advocate, and, as it seemed to me, of a not over fair one. For instance, dwelling on what was called the "Executive document,"[1] where it said "show this to Charles and John," Mr. Justice Fitzgerald read to the jurors "show this to Charles Kickham and John O'Leary," giving no inkling at first of the fact that he was interpreting and not quoting, and when this was pointed out to him, at my suggestion, by Dowse, he simply said that what he read (or rather read into it) was what the thing meant. But enough about Mr. Justice Fitzgerald. His charge matters little at this distance of time save as an example of how they manage these things in Ireland, or indeed in England either, where Irish political prisoners are concerned.

But to end my plain, unvarnished, and certainly unimaginative story. To bring myself personally on the scene, and then to have done with this legal business, and practically with my "recollections" altogether. The trial lasted from Friday, the 1st, up to Wednesday, the 6th

[1] This was a paper, written by Stephens and found in Luby's house, entrusting the government of the organization to Luby, Kickham, and myself during his absence in America. This document, though known to me, was never seen by me, and was not even known to Kickham, as no need for acting upon it had arisen.

of December, when I was found guilty, and the same measure meted out to me as to Luby—that was, twenty years' penal servitude. I give here what I am reported to have said, and what indeed I did say, substantially if not textually, why sentence should not be pronounced upon me, and the reader can judge for himself whether I was "labouring under much excitement," as the same pictorial person to whom I have before alluded says I was. Excited I no doubt was, but excessively I think not.

"I was not wholly unprepared for this verdict because I felt that the Government which could so safely pack the Bench could not fail to make sure of its verdict."

Mr. Justice FITZGERALD: "We are willing to hear anything in reason from you, but we cannot allow language of that kind to be used."

Mr. O'LEARY: "My friend Mr. Luby did not wish to touch on this matter from a natural fear lest he should do any harm to the other political prisoners, but there can be little fear of that now, for a jury has been found to convict me of this conspiracy upon the evidence. Mr. Luby admitted that he was technically guilty according to British law, but I say that it is only by the most tortured interpretation that these men could make out their case against me. With reference to this conspiracy there has been much misapprehension in Ireland, and serious misapprehension. Mr. Justice Keogh said in his charge against Mr. Luby that men would be always found ready for money, or for some other motive, to place themselves at the disposal of the Government; but I think the men who have been generally bought in this way, and who certainly make the best of the bargain, were agitators, not rebels. I have to say one word in reference to the foul charge upon which that miserable man Barry has made me responsible."

Mr. Justice FITZGERALD: "We cannot allow that tone of observation."

Mr. O'LEARY continued: "That man has charged me—I need not defend myself or my friends from the charge, I shall merely denounce the moral assassin. Mr. Justice Keogh the other day spoke of revolutions, and administered a lecture to Mr. Luby. He spoke of cattle being driven away, and of houses being burned down, that men would be killed, and so on. I would like to know if all that does not apply to war as well as to revolution. One word more, and I shall have done. I have been found guilty of treason or treason-felony. Treason is a foul crime. The poet Dante consigned traitors to, I believe, the ninth circle of hell, but what kind of traitors? Traitors against king, against country, against friends and benefactors. England is not my country; I have betrayed no friend, no benefactor. Sydney and Emmet were legal traitors. Jeffreys was a loyal man, and so was Norbury. I leave the matter there."

I might perhaps leave the matter there now too, and there, or here, I shall nearly leave it. I have only to add to what I said, some pages back, about Mr. Barry, that he looked perfectly astounded at my onslaught upon him, apparently amazed rather than indignant, and I remember that I thought this to his credit at the time. He clearly felt what I said; which, I think, is more than would have been the case, under similar circumstances, with his colleagues Lawson and Sullivan.

The pictorial person, to whom I have alluded before, tells his readers, in a supremely sensational fashion, that I was "the occupant of a cell in Mountjoy prison" an hour after the close of my speech, and there I leave myself, unsensationally, for the present.

CHAPTER XXIX.

FINIS.

HAVING said, if far from all I had to say, at least all that I think it fit to say, upon that part of the Fenian movement in which my labours mainly lay, I might perhaps, at least so far as my own feeling is concerned, not unfittingly bring this book to a close. I have done with all that with which I had directly most to do; still, many matters remain, of which indeed I was by no means so great a part, though some not inconsiderable part I was, and I know that the reader will require, to some extent at least, to have his curiosity satisfied about these things. The difficulty is how to do this. People do well to be curious about all things, but they have to rest satisfied with being left ignorant of many. I have said more than once that I was not even attempting to write a "History of Fenianism," but only my own recollections of it. Many people may wish that I had thought of doing what I have not thought of, but they can have no just ground of offence against me for not finding in my book what I expressly warned them would not be in it. However, such satisfaction, great or little, as I can give to feelings which are after all only natural, it is no doubt my business, or a part of it, to give.

And perhaps this is as good a place as another to begin upon what I feel to be about the hardest part of my task. I have been told by more than one person, and notably by Sir Charles Gavan Duffy, that it will be expected of me to give some satisfactory account of what were the chances of success in Fenianism. Well, I am afraid I cannot satisfy him or many another on this subject. It is very hard often to say what is success or failure in any movement, and when you come to measure chances, whether prospectively or retrospectively, the question of temperament always comes actively into play. Sir Gavan Duffy himself, in the second volume of his history of the Young Ireland movement, has elaborately tried to do for that movement what he expects me to do for the Fenian one, and I hope he will excuse me for saying here that he has scarcely succeeded in convincing many readers that there was any appreciable chance, in '48, of separating Ireland from England. Not the less was the Young Ireland movement far from a failure. The Young Irelanders taught us, not only *not* to fear to speak of the men of '98, but to think and feel that the right thing to do was to imitate them and their methods. '98, '48 and '65 failed, in the literal sense of the word, but in spirit they have none of them failed. To them, and not to any intervening constitutional windbagism, is it due that Ireland is still at its heart's core firm to be free.[1]

[1] Of course I am quite conscious of the ambiguity of the word "free." Some people, as I write, think we are going to become

But if I must candidly confess—judging long after the time, in the coolness of my study and not in the heat and turmoil of action—that I cannot prove that we had any great chance of wresting Ireland from the grasp of England, I think I can give strong reasons to show that, under certain contingencies, we might have made a formidable fight, and that, even as it was, we made it manifest to England, or rather to the English ruling classes, that their power in Ireland rested upon somewhat insecure foundations.[1]

I have spoken incidentally, from time to time, of the Irish soldiers in the English army, giving some little personal experience of my own in '48, and talking generally of our success among them; but I must enter shortly but specifically upon this branch of my subject here, and then have done with it.

It was now to be proved beyond dispute that England could not in the least rely upon the Irish soldiers in her

free by the passing of a Bill, which its author tells us is meant to strengthen the Union between the two countries. Perhaps this Bill may give us such measure of freedom as we need, or at least the means of finally reaching such measure. I know not, but this I do know, that most assuredly it will not do so by strengthening the Union.

[1] A war with America, which did not look an improbable event then, whatever men may think now, might have made Ireland free, as a war with that country, with Russia, or with France *may still make her free*, and I may here tell my untransacting friends that, humanly speaking, freedom for us under any other conditions seems impossible. I may also tell opportunist Irishmen and deceiving or self-deceiving Englishmen that, in any of these three contingencies, that "Union of hearts," the creation of designing knaves and deceived fools, would crumble like a pack of cards. That "Union of hearts" may come some half-century hence, and, whether it comes or not, will depend not upon us but upon England.

army. During the earlier years of the organization no attempt was made to tamper with the soldiers, Stephens naturally thinking that any action in that direction besides being dangerous was altogether premature. Shortly, however, after the establishment of the paper, Rossa came across a soldier, of the name of Sullivan, presumably from his own part of the country, and this man he swore in, and Sullivan in his turn swore in several others. In or about the same time some policemen and some members of the fire brigade were taken into the organization. But there I believe the thing stopped for the time.

It was several months after that the real work with the army began, and it was commenced and carried on, during the greater part of the time, by a very peculiar character, a clansman of my own, named Patrick O'Leary, but popularly known as "The Pagan." This name he owed to the fact that he professed to hold the faith of his (somewhat remote) ancestors, whom he asserted to be entirely demoralized, that is, rendered unwarlike and so an easy prey to successive conquerors, by their conversion to Christianity. This was all perhaps not quite what the French calls serious, though "The Pagan" was himself quite serious about it. Indeed he was serious, not to say stern, about most things. His mode with the soldiers was simplicity itself. He first asked his man if he were an Irishman, then made his proposal directly, and immediately after proceeded to administer the oath. This operation was, I believe, generally performed in a public-house, among its adjuncts being a lecture on temperance, for "The Pagan" was himself during all this time a strict teetotaller. So the thing went on for about a year or so, when some thousands at least of soldiers must have been enrolled. I have no figures before me, nor are they, to my mind, needed. I have always understood, from everybody having to do with the matter, that there was simply no limit to the getting in of these soldiers, save the natural ones of time and opportunity.

The end, however, at last came for "The Pagan," some months before it came for all of us, when he was "given away" by a soldier at Athlone, and soon after sentenced to a term of penal servitude. The work, however, went on quite as effectually, and, I should say, a good deal more cautiously,[1] first under the guidance of a well-known member of the organization, named William Roantree, and afterwards under the better known John Devoy and others. But to cut this matter short, there was no branch of the service into which we had not an entrance, and in the more purely Irish regiments the feeling of loyalty—not to the English Queen but to their own country—was almost universal. I was told, in prison, by Sergeant McCarthy—a fine type I may say, *en passant*, of the trained soldier and the true Irishman—that it was well known to the officers of one of the Irish regiments (88th, I think) stationed at Manchester, that their men were all Fenians in spirit if not in letter, and

[1] I am told by Luby that I said to him at the time that the extraordinary recklessness of "The Pagan" was rather an advantage in dealing with these soldiers, who were themselves mostly daring, and but too often rash.

that the only use made of the knowledge was to get the regiment packed off to India, or some other distant part of the Empire, as soon as possible.

So much for the soldiers. I do not know, and I do not greatly care, how my statements will strike my readers; my concern all through this book being to present my own opinions, feelings, and experiences, in no way modifying them to suit the varying palates of any possible public. And in this matter of the Irish soldiers my feeling is strong as death that, however useful their services may be abroad to England, at home she will always have to reckon with them as enemies.

As to what kind of impression we produced upon the police I am not in a position to say much. I think that any extensive tampering with them was discouraged by Stephens, as I should myself have discouraged it if I had had anything to say in the matter, as being too much in the nature of playing with edged tools. Some considerable effect was, however, produced upon the Dublin police. Two brothers Breslin, for instance, both I believe sergeants in that body, were arrested, and their arrest was the first thing that cast suspicion on their brother John, well known since in connection with the escape of Stephens and the Australian prisoners. Anyway, the conduct of these men towards us while in prison, whatever might be their political belief or want of belief, was kindness itself. Hence I could never in the least share some latter-day opinions, arising out of some Phœnix Park ruction, about the brutality of the

Dublin police. They are, as far as I could ever see, about as little brutal as any body of men can well be. They baton people when they are in danger of being themselves bludgeoned or stoned—and why shouldn't they? Of our dealings with the Constabulary I know still less. Many of these, however, I have heard of in America, and some of them, as notably General Corcoran, I have known and found quite as good Irishmen as others, and mostly above the average in intelligence. I do not care to dwell too long on, and I certainly do not wish to exaggerate at all, what was done, or might be done, either with the soldiers or the police. I have no doubt whatever myself on this subject, and the English Government, at least so far as the army was concerned, by numerous court martials and consequent convictions, did much to remove from the public mind any delusions that might have previously existed as to the feelings or opinions of Irish soldiers. With the police things are of course a little (or perhaps a good deal) different. They will never show the same disregard for consequences as soldiers, tending, both professionally and probably naturally, to the side of caution, but I think it may very safely be assumed that they are mostly one in sentiment and thought with the class of their countrymen from which they are taken.

But to come to the organization proper, and while I have still the question of fully trained men in my mind, I may say, *en passant*, that we had many men—how many it would be hard for me to tell—besides the soldiers who were soldiers—ex-army men, militiamen, policemen, and men who had served in the American war. And the mention of this last item reminds me of the fact that the close of that war set free for a fight in Ireland a practically unlimited number of soldiers of all ranks, full of military ardour, and burning with an unextinguishable hatred of England. Of course I do not need to be told that these men were far from the scene of action, but perhaps there are many who do need to be reminded that the question here involved is one largely of money. The elements have been rhetorically said to fight on the side of England, but they cannot help her in an age of steamers as they could in an age of sailing vessels. I am here only touching upon this branch of the Fenian question. It is not easy to bring men—especially armed men from America to Ireland, though I may add, *par parenthese*, that it would be far easier to bring the men and the arms separately. Still, a great many men—mostly officers—did come over, but I must leave it to more imaginative people to conjecture the number that might have come had funds been ample, and had there been no division[1] of counsels in the Irish-American ranks. Coming at last, after devious but not very lengthy windings, to the men at home, I have to remind the reader once more that I am giving, as far as possible, my own recollections, and as little as I can easily avoid anything that goes

[1] To my mind the Canadian policy was suicidal. We could not free Ireland by any possible military successes in Canada, while we could, and I have little doubt did, alienate American and even Irish-Canadian feeling.

much outside of them. Stephens and Luby[1] could say much directly on this head, which must come but indirectly from me. Still, recollections I have in abundance on this head, and many reflections, and these I shall proceed to present to the reader briefly, and when that is done, I believe I may consider my task is practically at an end.

Up to the time of the starting of the paper, towards the close of the year '63, the organization was comparatively limited in numbers, and more or less confined to certain localities. It was strong in the city of Dublin and in the adjoining counties, in Kilkenny, Cork, Kerry, and other parts of the East and South; in fact, it might be said to be mainly situated in Leinster and Munster. The limitation both as to numbers and places was, I am thoroughly convinced, altogether due to the lack of money and the consequent difficulty in finding agents, or rather in paying them. And talking of paying, I may say that far the largest part of the work was done gratuitously all along. But most of our men were poor, nearly all having to earn their daily bread, and so their propagandism was largely exercised on Sundays, and necessarily mostly ranging over small areas. What could be done from Dublin, Cork, or other large or small centres, was done, and done zealously.

[1] Indeed, humanly speaking, I have little doubt but Luby will be heard, and heard effectually, on this and many other Fenian matters in the near future. Indeed, I have by me, as I write, much matter of his which needs but putting into shape. Perhaps it is one of many sins in connection with this book of my own, that I am incidentally keeping Luby's book back.

But breaking up new ground, especially in regions more or less distant from existing organizations, was difficult. Much was of course effected by the various journeys of Stephens and Luby, but these were comparatively "few and far between," constantly hindered and hampered by that perpetual obstacle to all enterprise—the want of money.

But in the early *Irish People* times, and constantly from that to the end, there was a vast change for the better. The organization grew rapidly and spread more or less over all the land, as well as in England and Scotland too. I have mentioned the names of John Nolan and of Edward Duffy before, and said something of their doings in the North and West, but I must dwell at greater length here both upon the men and their exertions. They may be said to have opened up Ulster and Connaught to the organization. Small incursions had been made into these provinces before, but now for the first time was the ground to be thoroughly worked.

John Nolan was a commercial traveller, and so exceptionally well situated to do good work for us while carrying on his ordinary avocations. Anyway, he did the work, and did it so well, that before the end, as far as I could gather at the time, Ulster was well in line with the other provinces.

With Duffy and Connaught things went equally well, or rather still better, for, before Duffy found his way to a prison cell and a felon's grave, he left Connaught in probably as good a state of preparation as Munster, and most likely somewhat in advance of either Leinster or Ulster.

Of course, in the original seats of strength—in Dublin, Cork, and elsewhere—the organization went on growing wider and firmer from day to day, the numbers were increasing and hopes growing higher with our gathering strength and the general aspect of affairs. Another considerable advance made during this time, dating roughly from the coming into being of the paper, was the getting into the organization of a somewhat better class of young men,[1] that is, better socially and educationally, though probably mostly not so much better intellectually, and morally I think the men we had all along were about as high as human nature will allow masses of men ever to be. Among these young men it is needless to give any names. Many of them have gone into far other paths since, and would not thank me for recalling what they may have come to look upon as the errors of their youth. One family of young men, however, I can recall with pleasure and with pride. They have most of them long since gone to their fathers, but such of them as still remain are little likely to be other than proud of their patriotic record. I am of course alluding to the young O'Donovans, the sons of the great Irish scholar, and all very considerable scholars themselves, and one

[1] Later on we drew largely upon a better class still, both of the young and the middle-aged, but that was at a time outside of the range of my recollections, and, queerly enough, at a time when one would have least expected—that is, after our imprisonment in '65, and even after what might fairly be considered the collapse of the movement in '67.

of them at least,[1] Edmond, the well-known war correspondent, a very considerable writer too. At this time, however, Edmond's mind seemed to take rather a scientific than a literary direction, but I suppose this was due rather to the supposed exigencies of the situation than to any other cause. Anyway, he taught the men many practical and useful matters in a sort of a military school of which he was the guiding spirit, but which was much frequented and much admired by many of the more active and more intelligent among the Dublin young men.

Talking of these young men of a later day reminds me of saying a few words parenthetically about the class of young men from which we drew largely all along. Snobbish people have been in the habit of sneering at the servant boys, farm labourers, and the like, whom they suppose to have given us all (or nearly all) our numerical strength, as at the American servant girls from whom we are supposed to have derived most of our funds. Well, I do not in the least desire to deny that our movement was mainly one of the masses and not of the classes,[2] though in no sense opposed to any class or creed of our countrymen. However, these servant boys and labourers, though I am happy to say we had many of them, were

[1] I add the qualifying "at least" because I think John, the eldest of the brothers, was also a very good writer, but he wrote little; while Willie, a very good scholar and able man, wrote much, but I think not well.

[2] We felt, with our great forerunner Wolfe Tone, that, "if the men of property will have nothing to do with us, we must fall back upon that highly respectable class of the community, the men of no property."

not, in proportion to their numbers, more strongly represented in our ranks than other sections of the community. If I were to judge from my own experience, and from what I could ever gather, I should say that we had a greater proportion of shopmen, of all possible grades in the various establishments, and of all possible kinds of shops, from the country shebeen to the monster houses of Dublin, Cork, and the other large cities. In these last we had from the beginning and all along some of our best workers, and in the end seem to have absorbed nearly the whole *personnel* of many of these big houses.

I have dwelt upon our strength among the shopmen at the greater length because that body of young men, especially in certain of its branches, is, absurdly enough, supposed to be somewhat effeminate, and also because, judging always from my personal experience, I should say that the men in the shops, as compared with the men in the workshops, were relatively more important in '65 than in '48. But, of course, these last also were most numerous in our movement, as they have been in all national movements, and we had had them of all grades too, from the humblest (I use the epithet, applied to himself, of my poor friend and fellow-prisoner, Terry Byrne) shoemaker in his garret to the comparatively prosperous clerk of works or builder.

Shopkeepers we had too, but chiefly in the smaller towns, or, when in the large towns, of the smaller sort. Farmers we had, of course, too, most of whom, I grant, were small ones. But not all. O'Neill Crowley, for instance, the hero of Kilcloony Wood, was, I understand, a very extensive farmer. But in making all these concessions to our snobbish critics, I do not want to go too far. The shopkeepers and farmers in possession were generally elderly men, and very often, when we had not themselves, we had their sons. Besides, as I have said more than once in this book, I believe your middle class man, whether of the higher or the lower middle class, is mostly the least altruistic of men. I need scarcely say what our upper classes are. I can only fondly hope that they may some time or other come, or return, to some sense of duty to their country. Meantime the so-called lower classes—the masses—are the backbone of the country; for many purposes, and indeed, I think, for nearly all self-sacrificing ones, they are the country. 'Tis sad that this should be so; perhaps even fatal while it is so, but there is no use in blinking the fact. Let our critics then get such comfort as they can from my confession that our movement was mainly one of the masses, not against the classes, but unfortunately without them. But there is another side, if not many other sides, to this question of *our* masses. There are masses of Irishmen—happily, if, alas! also unhappily—abroad as well as at home; and by abroad I most certainly mean England, Scotland and Wales, as well as America, Australia, and the rest of the world. England has the Irish enemy confronting her in every quarter of the globe.[1]

[1] These may seem strange words to many when this book makes its appearance. I write them, after reading my morning paper,

I have said much all along of the direct aid we got from our countrymen in America, but I must dwell somewhat on the powerful indirect aid they might have given us. Neither in O'Connell's time, nor in the Young Ireland period, but only, if not by and through Fenianism, at least during Fenianism, was it first shown what a powerful factor in Irish politics the Irish in America had become.

At the close of the American War there were 200,000 disbanded Irish soldiers, all eager for any fray,[1] but gasping to be at the throat of England. I have refused to enter into any detailed speculation as to the number of these men who could, under certain conditions, find their way to Ireland. One contingency I must, however, consider for a moment, and that is one which is ever present in the minds of Irish Nationalists. War between America and England may be an unlikely event—how much or how little so it is hard to say; but the latter country should never forget that it is ever the dearest heart-wish of the millions of Irish in the States. Neither should it be forgotten that, however we may view the matter now, war did not seem so unlikely at the time of which I am writing. The sanguine among

where I find our English friends and enemies fighting over our bodies, searching, seeking, but alas! I fear, finding not; all equally ignoring the fact that it will never be well with us till they see (or are made to see) their way to leaving us alone.

[1] "L'Irlandais," said Frederick the Great," "se batte, pour le plaisir de se battre." I do not quote this saying because I am particularly proud of our fondness for fighting, but 'tis an element in our composition which must be taken into account both by our friends and our enemies.

us—and naturally most of us were sanguine, or we should not have been what we were—might even be excused for thinking it likely. And the Irish in America might easily be more hopeful still, conscious as they must have been how much they could themselves do to fan into a flame the smouldering sparks—and they seemed numerous enough—of discontent still rankling in the American breast. Had the *Alabama* difficulty but then come to the front, what might not these Irish millions have done to arouse or exasperate popular feeling? and there were the hundreds of thousands of hands, with hearts behind them, ever ready and willing instruments for use against England.

But enough. There was no war, but the danger was ever there for England as the hope for Ireland. *And it is there still.* There is not as yet even a pretence of a union of hearts on the part of the Irish in America, and as to union of hearts at home, perhaps the less said the soonest mended. In trying to be purely retrospective, I find it almost impossible to keep the present from peeping in occasionally. Times change and men change with them, but there is a terrible continuity in things Irish, and certain Irishmen, like myself, for example, while undergoing many mental and moral metamorphoses, as the years roll on, still remain very much the same in opinion as regards things English and Irish, and very nearly altogether the same in feeling.

But the question is not in the least either what I am or others may be, but how men and things stood in Ireland in '65.

In seeking to bring this narrative to a close, I have dealt up to this with more or less exterior sides of the movement—the soldiers and police, the Irish in America and elsewhere, the chances of a war between the United States and England, and the like; but all these actualities and possibilities, at least so far as our great object was concerned, came to nothing in the long run. The red was still above the green, and there it has remained ever since, and there, I fear, it is destined to remain for some indefinite time to come. In how far we could have made things other than they were, if we had been wiser and better, I know not, and I think it would not be easy for anybody to know. Here again, any way, as so often before "in our old island, story," we have one more instance of the proverbial good luck of England and the proverbial ill luck of Ireland, or, if the reader prefers to have it put so, of the will of God. It is of course open to people to think that all things in this world are as they should be, and that they could not be other than they are; as it is also equally open to them to think that a certain person's children have that certain person's luck. But what I think it is perfectly ridiculous for any set of Irishmen to believe is, that, if any people fail to reach the goal, they prove thereby that they were never on the right path. All Irish efforts to attain freedom, or even a partial measure of freedom, have failed. But Fenianism, in the mere material sense even, did not altogether fail. It has been often pointed out by others, and by myself, I think, if not in this book, at least somewhere, that Fenianism disestablished the Irish Church and brought about the passing of the first Land Act. To be sure Fenianism did not seek to do either of these things, but that is beside the question. The gist of the matter lies in the fact that even so-called good measures are mostly not due to oratory or agitation, but rather to silent action.

So much, *en passant*, for the mere material side of things, but matter is not everything. Nations, any more than individuals, live not by bread alone. It was a proud and not undeserved boast of the Young Irelanders that they "brought a soul back into Eiré," but before Fenianism arose that soul had fled. Fenianism brought it back again, teaching men to sacrifice themselves for Ireland instead of selling themselves and Ireland to England. But we failed, and our spirit fled from the land, and then, in the vicious circle we seem to be for ever describing, came back the old agitating methods and but too much of the spirit of the old agitating men, leaving us as far as ever from freedom and apparently, or rather certainly for the moment, without that spirit which, though it may fail to gain freedom, alone deserves it.

But that spirit is not dead (for the soul of a nation, any more than of an individual, cannot die) but merely sleepeth, and if there be men still in Ireland, and still more boys growing into men, willing to strive and struggle and sacrifice, if needs be, liberty or life for Ireland, to Fenianism more than to aught else is that spirit and feeling due.

INDEX.

N.

O.

P.

PRINTED BY GILBERT AND RIVINGTON, LD., ST. JOHN'S HOUSE, CLERKENWELL, E.C.

CPSIA information can be obtained
at www.ICGtesting.com
Printed in the USA
BVHW042348150620
581544BV00003B/115

9 781376 309553